'Imagine your team
working with the SPEED,
purpose and **intensity**
of a pit team.'

www.GrowthPitstop.com

ISBN: 978-1-907725-08-1

CONTENTS

*Dedicated to Michael Schumacher
and his family.*

*My philosophy is never to think you have achieved it!
Always looking for the millimeters/seconds...
... find it on lap 50 of the third day!*
Michael Schumacher[1]

*'You never really know how quick you are
before you reach F1™.'*

Jean Alesi, Driver[2]

F1™, FORMULA ONE™ and FORMULA 1™ are trademarks of Formula One™ Licensing BV, a Formula One™ group company. They are used in good faith in accordance with 'Nominative Fair Use' to describe the qualities and characteristics of these highly unique and special events / sports / pursuits.

The Performance Pitstop™ or Growth Pitstop™ is <u>not</u> affiliated with or has <u>not</u> been endorsed or sponsored by Formula One™ in any manner, nor licensed any intellectual property for use in this book.

The Performance Pitstop™, The Growth Pitstop™, P2P Metric™, Pitstop Analytics™ and RevenueTrack™ are registered marks of The ASG Group.

Other trademarks referenced, including: Scuderia Ferrari F1™, Lotus F1™, NASCAR™, Goolge™, Mercedes™, Red Bull™ and Nike™ are the registered trademarks of the respective organizations.

INTRODUCTION

What percentage of your organization or team's full potential is presently being exploited? That simple yet powerful question is a great place to start a conversation about performance. Indeed, it is such a powerful question that, of all the possible openings to this book, we wanted to begin with it. So here it is again:

What % of your organization/team's <u>full</u> potential is presently being exploited?

(circle the point on the scale below)

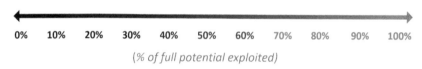

| 0% | 10% | 20% | 30% | 40% | 50% | 60% | 70% | 80% | 90% | 100% |

(% of full potential exploited)

We call this the BIG question, because it goes to the heart of the performance debate. It is also a test. If the BIG performance question gets you excited, frustrated, or even curious then read on. However, if the BIG question leaves you cold this is probably not the book or approach for you – at least not at this time. This book has been specifically written for those who are **concerned with, or responsible for; the performance** and potential of an organization, business in unit or team.

YOUR NEXT 5%, 10% OR 15%

Pitstop to Perform™ will help you to:

- **Scientifically assess** the performance potential of your organization, business unit or team, specifically its P2P Metric™ (see panel below).

- **Systematically exploit** the next 5%, 10%, 15% or your organization, business unit or team's full potential – called Performance Gains.

- **Tackle any barriers** (called Performance Losses) preventing your team spending more time in the Zone of Peak Performance™.

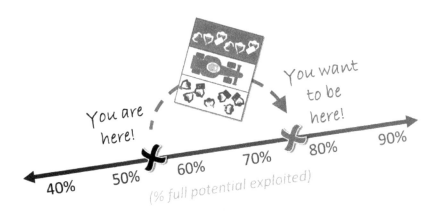

The P2P Metric™ is the ratio of performance to potential for an organization, business unit or team. Just like an organization's Net Promoter Score™[3] or the Unemployment Rate for an economy, it is a yardstick against which performance can be measured, adjusted and monitored over time – one that enables internal and external comparison too.

YOUR FULL POTENTIAL

For more than a decade we have been asking the BIG performance question of managers and their teams. We have done it thousands of times across 12 industries in 47 markets. While the percentage answers vary – typically falling somewhere between 40% and 70% - the conclusion is always the same: there is lots of un-tapped potential. It exists within almost every organization and team.

Imagine your organization, business unit or team in the Zone of...

Peak Performance

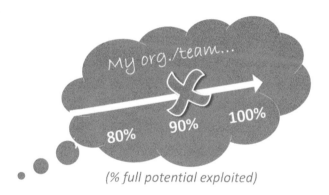

(% full potential exploited)

For people to be operating significantly below their full potential could be seen as a major performance loss - a loss of talent, opportunity and resources. However, viewed from a positive perspective it also offers the promise of significant future performance gains. Indeed, if only a small proportion of the untapped potential within organizations and teams was exploited **it could transform organizations, even societies**. It is this realization, from early in our research, that has been our driving purpose. This is what has inspired us to publish this book – the sixth in a series.

YOUR PERFORMANCE LOSSES

There are many reasons why organizations, business units and teams leave so much potential unexploited. There are situational and structural factors, including culture, leadership, environment and strategy. There are also issues of skills, attitudes and behaviors. We have catalogued, classified, measured and modelled the barriers to peak performance in all their real-world complexity – up to 200 of them in total! We use the term 'Performance Losses' to describe them – it is a deliberate effort to **overcome the traditional challenges of bridging the gap between performance and potential.**

MODELLING PERFORMANCE POTENTIAL

Pitstop to Perform™ is a global breakthrough in terms of measuring, modelling and predicting performance and potential. This enables teams to **transform performance losses into measurable gains, typically in the range of 7-25%.** Central to this is the pitstop meta-model, performance algorithm and a powerful P2P Metric™ (ratio of performance to potential).

Pitstop to Perform™ is the first in the world to integrate behavioural dynamics and organizational/team design with business strategy and execution. It is also the first to transform performance losses into measurable gains.

RESEARCHING PERFORMANCE

Pitstop to Perform™ is based on extensive research into 'performance losses' within business units and teams in some of the world's biggest and best corporations. That includes business units and teams within; Great West Life Co., GE, IBM, 3M and Pfizer. The research is summarized below:

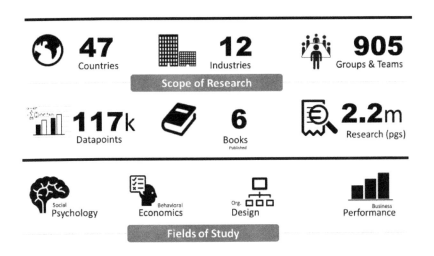

The Pitstop Meta-model leverages insights from the performance-obsessed arena of F1™ to bring to life the latest research from social psychology, behavioural economics, organizational design and business leadership.

NAVIGATING THIS BOOK

In the first two sections we are going to guide you through the process of **diagnosing the performance and potential of your organization, business unit or team**. In so doing we map your business unit or team to a particular Zone of Performance (Section 1) and identify those factors limiting its potential (Section 2).

When it comes to performance looking back at what has happened is not enough – it is essential to look to the future. That is what happens in Sections 3 to 8 where we explore how to **model and predict the performance of your organization, business unit or team** using the power of the Pitstop Meta-model.

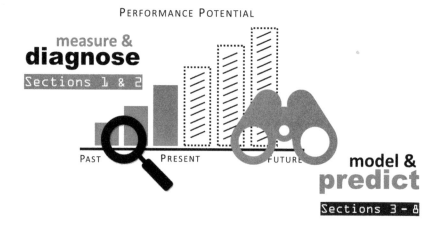

INSPIRED BY F1™

If you bought this book because you are a fan of Formula 1™ you won't be disappointed. From Section 3 onwards we will leverage insights and inspiration from F1™ to build a next generation model of performance.

The racetrack is a popular metaphor for the demands of competing in an increasingly competitive and fast changing business environment.

Here are just some of the words that are most commonly associated with F1™[4]. Most, if not all of them, have direct relevance to the world of business.

The real purpose of bringing F1™ into this book is to get you thinking in a new way about a topic that can be difficult. The objective is a psychological one - to de-personalize and de-politicize the issue of performance, thereby generating new openness, energy and engagement. The technical term for this is Cognitive Reframing – creating a way of viewing and experiencing events, ideas, concepts and emotions to find more positive alternatives. So, you don't need to be interested in fast cars and Champagne to benefit.

ENGAGE WITH US

If you have any ideas or questions about your organization's performance journey (or that of your clients), please contact us at support@growthpitstop.com. Also, please visit us online at www.GrowthPitstop.com for:

Pitstop Analytics™

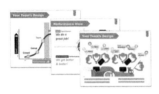

Assess the performance potential of your team using Pitstop Analytics™.

Workshop Kits

Everything you need to run a pitstop workshop with your team in one box.

Pitstop Posters

Keep the Pitstop Meta-model™ front of mind with posters for your office.

Research Insights

Access insights & tools on any part of the meta-model (e.g Right People).

www.GrowthPitstop.com/shop

SECTION 1

THE BIG QUESTION

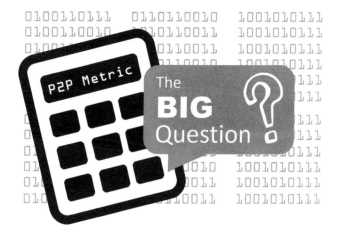

INTRODUCTION

This Section is all about Peak Performance – what it is and how it is measured. More specifically, it is about how close your organization, business unit or team is to realizing Peak Performance.

Over the coming pages we will measure not just the performance of your team, but its potential too. In so doing we will seek to overcome many of the limitations in how performance has traditionally been measured, managed and even discussed.

PERFORMANCE DIAGNOSIS

Let's jump straight into our diagnosis of performance with the BIG question.

What % of your organization's

full potential

is presently being exploited?

(circle the point on the scale below)

0%   10%   20%   30%   40%   50%   60%   70%   80%   90%   100%

(% of full potential exploited)

On the surface the BIG question seems straight-forward, but dig deeper and a hidden layer of complexity is revealed. As we will examine, the BIG question:

- Gathers an important piece of performance data – the ratio of performance to potential, called the P2P Metric™.
- Acts as a performance test – a telling test of both mindset and psychology[5].

The BIG question is not just a question about performance. It is about performance and potential, or what we call 'performance potential'. That is what your team can and should achieve – not just what it has done or failed to do. So, it is future-focused and positive - something that is vital if people are to strive for Peak Performance.

The Growth Pitstop™ Community works with many large and successful corporations - leaders in their industries and household names - they dominate markets, launch exciting products and out-pace their competitors. But look within those organizations and you will find leaders and teams that are performing way below their potential.   Here is the paradox - **many organizations are meeting their targets, while a great number of their people are operating at between 55% and 74% of what they are capable of**[6]. That is why we say 'performance' and 'performance potential' are two separate things. The first concerns the organization and 'what is'. The second concerns leaders and teams and 'what could be'.

PUTTING IT TO WORK

The BIG performance question can be asked at any level; the organization overall, or more powerfully at the level of a business unit / function, team and individual[7].

BIG Q: Where will you focus?

What % of your Organization's / Business Unit's / Department's / Function's / Team / Group's / Individual's / Personal full potential is being exploited?

0% 10% 20% ... 60% 70% 80% 90% 100%

At the opening of the section, we asked the BIG question for your organization overall. That is a good place to start. However, while interesting it may hide as much as it reveals. To really make the BIG question meaningful a more granular analysis is required[8]. That means viewing the organization as a portfolio of business units, functions and regions – each with its own level of performance and potential. So, let's apply the BIG question across the organizational portfolio as in the example shown overleaf.

This data is from a real organization, however we have disguised its identity to protect confidentiality. As the diagram shows, ACME's P2P Metric™ (ratio of performance to potential) varies greatly by business unit and region.

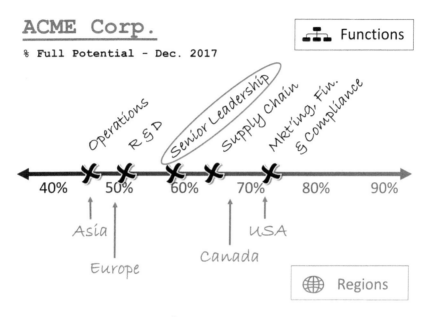

ACME Corp. — Functions

% Full Potential - Dec. 2017

Operations R & D Senior Leadership Supply Chain Mkt'ing, Fin. & Compliance

40%   50%   60%   70%   80%   90%

Asia
Europe
Canada
USA

Regions

Thinking like a strategist[9] this 'portfolio' analysis of the BIG question illuminates many pockets of performance potential. However, ACME's CEO immediately circled the Senior Leadership Team as his primary focus of attention – putting it succintly he proclaimed 'they are the people who I depend upon to make it all happen'. Now, with a particular team selected the BIG question could generate a more granular analysis.

Where would you like to focus? Using the blank page overleaf complete the portfolio analysis of the BIG question (as above) for your organization's key business units or functions and then focus on a specific business unit or team that is particularly important to your success and that of your organization[10].

Apply the BIG question across your organizational portfolio - applying it to its key business units, functions and teams (as in the example on the previous page)

% Full Potential Exploited

Date : _____

0% 10% 20% 30% 40% 50% 60% 70% 80% 90% 100%

Functions

Regions

UNIT OR TEAM PERFORMANCE

The debate about performance can feel abstract when it is at the level of an organization or portfolio. Making it real requires a more granular analysis of performance potential. For example, the CEO above rated his Senior Leadership Team at 60% overall, but this figure tells only part of the story. To really understand the performance potential of the Senior Leadership Team (SLT) requires deconstructing the average. For example, the team's performance in respect of each of its top priorities is shown in the next diagram.

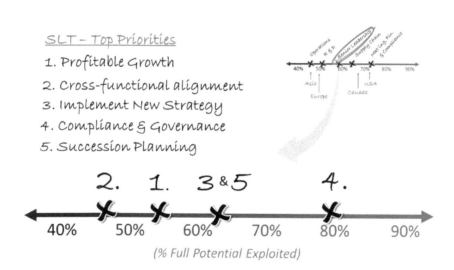

SLT – Top Priorities

1. Profitable Growth
2. Cross-functional alignment
3. Implement New Strategy
4. Compliance & Governance
5. Succession Planning

(% Full Potential Exploited)

This team is performing well in some areas, but is underperforming in others – notably the CEO rated performance in respect of the top two priorities at between just 45% and 55% of where it could be.

How do I get my P2P Metric™?

How do you know if your answer to the BIG question is accurate? Could you be over confident about your team's performance or perhaps underestimating its true potential? Well, there is a data-driven answer to the BIG question, called the P2P Metric™. This is the ratio of performance to potential calculated scientifically based on 186 performance variables as measured by the Pitstop Analytics™ platform. The result is an accurate measure of performance and potential at the level of the organization, business unit or team. This is accompanied by a thorough diagnosis of performance losses, as well as predictive modelling of performance gains (as examined in the next section). Why you need to know your P2P Metric™ and more information on the Pitstop Performance Analytics™ can be found in the Appendix.

Next the CEO applied the BIG question across the members of the team. This resulted in more revelations as shown below.

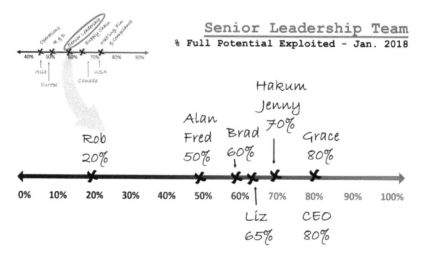

With individual P2P Metrics™ ranging from 20% to 80%, some team members are clearly realizing more of their potential than others. Here are some of the reasons why this type of analysis is important:

(a) Performance is personal. Just as each team member has unique talents and abilities, what 100% or even Peak Performance (a term we will explain shortly) means is likely to be different for each person. In this example Grace's peak performance is different from Brad's or Jenny's - so too are the requirements of unlocking it[11].

(b) Performance is situational and there are many external factors at play. For example:

- Fred (at 50%) is presently stuck in the wrong role – the work he is doing is not what he joined for, enjoys or is suited to[12].

- Alan (also at 50%) is under pressure in his domestic life due to the illness of his spouse[13].

(c) Performance is both Individual & Collective. In most organizations the model of performance is focused on the individual[14]. Yet, as this team reveals there is no separating individual and collective performance[15]. In the example above, Grace is a high performer - hired based on her impressive resume and list of achievements in previous roles. But what will happen when she joins a team where everybody else is performing at a lower level and 3 people are performing below 50%? Performance can be contagious – the question is: Will Grace inspire others to higher levels or performance, or alternatively sink to their level?

A word of caution: Take care as you complete this analysis and don't let personalities or politics distract you. Although it is tempting to point the finger at certain individuals and their behaviors, this is a fundamental error.[16] It results in short term fixes that tackle only the symptoms, leaving the underlying patterns or problems unresolved. With 3 of the 9 members of this Senior Leadership Team performing below 55%, the problem runs deeper than a few named individuals[17]. There are systemic factors at play including the culture of the organization, the style of the leader and past failed attempts at restructuring. Leaders who want to redefine and drive performance must be able to identify and tackle such systemic or underlying causes of under-performance. They must be good systems thinkers – as we will explore in the next section[18].

PERFORMANCE IS PERSONAL

The juxtaposition of performance and potential can be seen at all levels within an organization or team. However, as one of our colleagues is fond of saying; 'performance begins at home'[19]. In other words, leaders should first look to their own performance potential, before looking to others. So, take a moment and reflect on the personal version of the BIG Question:

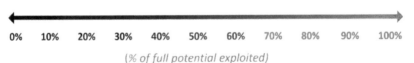

What % of your own <u>full</u> potential is presently being exploited?

(circle ✐ the point on the scale below)

0%   10%   20%   30%   40%   50%   60%   70%   80%   90%   100%

(% of full potential exploited)

Note the word 'presently' in the BIG question. That is important because the answer is situational. Today you may be performing at 80%, but falling to 60% at the end of the month because you have been on 3 long-haul flights in 4 weeks. So, write today's date beside your answer on the scale above. Come back time and again to ask the BIG question, tracking any trends and adapting accordingly. Before you move on, why not explore what % of your full potential others think that you are presently exploiting.

BEHIND THE NUMBER

Now that you are familiar with the BIG question it is a good time to reveal that it actually has two parts. The first part is to pick the percentage on the scale – as you have done already. The second is to explain the thinking behind that figure. To do this we will borrow from a recent psychological paper20 and explore your team's present position in terms of:

 - **Factors that are propelling you or your team <u>forward</u>** in terms of performance (and have brought it to its present position e.g. 65%), you can think of these as Tailwinds (i.e. a wind that blows in the direction of travel thereby increasing its momentum).

- **Factors that are holding your team performance <u>back</u>** (from reaching 75%, 85% or more) - you can think of these as Headwinds (i.e. a wind that blows against the direction of travel, thereby slowing progress).

Use the panels overleaf to identify the tailwinds and headwinds for yourself or your team. This is a page you might like to copy – asking others to share their views and using it every time you see the BIG question.

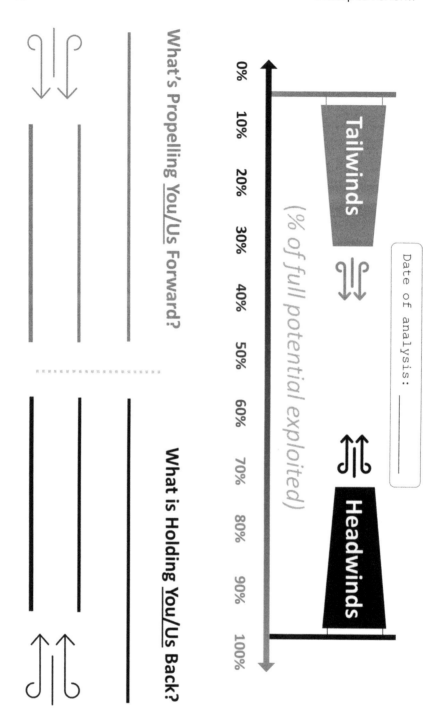

What's Propelling You/Us Forward?

What is Holding You/Us Back?

Date of analysis: _____

(% of full potential exploited)

Tailwinds

Headwinds

0% 10% 20% 30% 40% 50% 60% 70% 80% 90% 100%

Engaging Multiple Perspectives

Ask the BIG question of your colleagues and peers. The more perspectives you get the clearer the picture of performance potential will become. Here is an example of just how performance potential can vary.

The diagram above plots performance potential for the 48 managers below the Senior Leadership Team from our earlier example. As this page (generated by the Pitstop Analytics™) shows most executives fall outside the Zone of Peak Performance™.

PERFORMING IN THE 75% ZONE

When a team is operating at 75% or more of its 'full' potential we describe it as being 'in the zone' or more specifically 'in the Zone of Peak Performance™'. This requires some further explanation – in particular those with curious minds will ask:

- What is meant by 'full' potential?
- Why the figure of 75%?

Let's answer each of these questions in turn.

(a) What is meant by full potential?

That is a great question, to which the one-line answer is; 'that's what the individual, unit or team is capable of'. Answering the BIG question requires making a judgment as to what your team and its members are capable of. It also requires considering obstacles and constraints both internal and external, imagined and real. To take a motor racing example, there is no point in having a Ferrari and driving it at 61 km/hr. If on the other hand, it is a smart car you are driving, then 61km/hr may be a fine speed and near to the car's full potential.

(b) Why the figure of 75%?

Some people are surprised that the Zone of Peak Performance™ starts at just 75% - for them this seems under-ambitious. Well, as one member of the pitstop partner community argues - an individual or team can never achieve 100%. As an experienced leadership coach, he encourages leaders to aim for a more realistic 80% or 90% and suggests (with sustainability in mind) that individuals and teams can only expect to operate at those levels 80-90% of the time. That is interesting because if you do the math, operating at 90% for 80% of the time would equate to an overall performance level of 72%. Hence, the P2P Metric™ of 75%+ is a realistic and yet challenging threshold for the Zone of Peak Performance™.

Performing at the Limit

Technically speaking a F1™ racing car is capable of speeds in excess of 400 km/ph. However, cars can only perform at a fraction of their potential velocity due to safety regulations, track conditions, driver skill and of course the requirements of maintaining traction while accelerating around sharp corners. As seasoned race champion Ross Bentley points out the job description for the professional race driver is a simple one: "to drive the car at the limit, no more no less."[21] The reality for race drivers, as well as executives, is that there is always some limit and it is these limits that test the driver, car and team.

> *You have to have an inbuilt need to push the car to the limit and the fearlessness that comes with it.*
> Jenson Button[22]

PERFORMING IN THE 75% ZONE

The 75%+ Zone is the zenith of performance. It is the equivalent of 'Formula One™' in motor racing - competitive, innovative and driven by excellence. But it is not for everybody, just the elite - those who are most passionate, disciplined and determined.

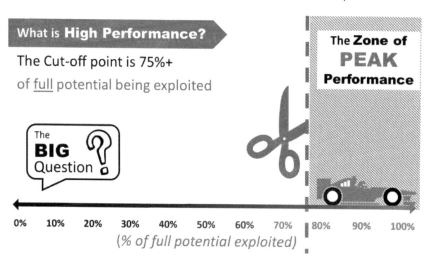

Here are just some of the reasons why the Zone of Peak Performance™ is not a crowed space:

1. There is a high price to be paid for entry to the Peak Zone. It demands real effort, discipline and sacrifice. It also requires trust, self-belief, risk-taking, pushing the limits and at times danger. While this is the place for those obsessed with winning, it is paved with frustration, as well as ambition. Here the moments of celebration and self-satisfaction are often out-numbered by those of impatience, restlessness and frustration. Peak performance requires grit and the ability to make short term sacrifice for the prospect of longer term gain[23].

Who are the peak performers of tomorrow? The peak potentials if you like. What are the leadership environmental and other factors that can propel people into the Zone of Peak Performance™ and more importantly keep them there?

2. It is difficult (if not impossible) to mandate or compel peak performance. Setting high standards / expectations is important, but for people to dig deep within themselves requires a passion-fuelled commitment.

3. This is a zone of heat, noise and friction. Those who are 'in the zone' are demanding of themselves and others. They are often Type A personalities with high standards and impatience[24]. But their obsessive task focus can make them poor team players.

4. There is no standing still - sustaining peak performance is a challenge. It requires continuous improvement and innovation, plus the ability to learn from mistakes.

5. The solo-run is common. In the race for progress other people are often left behind. For peak performers, the slow majority can be an obstacle to progress. To everybody else, peak performers can seem impatient, egotistical and selfish.

There are moments of peak performance within every team. Instances when extraordinary discipline, creativity and perhaps even genius can be seen. In most cases these are fleeting however. So much so that they often go unrecognized. The challenge is to have more of these peak moments, to appreciate, celebrate and reward them. Thereby encouraging people to spend more time 'in the zone' - making peak performance more a habit and mode of working, than an accident. List some moments of peak performance you have recently witnessed.

---

6. Crashes and burnouts are common. The peak zone doesn't have a slow lane – those who are in it can find it difficult to relax and regularly flirt with burnout. But performance and well-being are two sides of the same coin and in the long run you cannot have one without the other[25].

> *Motor racing is a sport that brings people to the limit: men and machine...*
> Ayrton Senna[26]

IN OR OUT OF THE ZONE?

Remember the CEO's Leadership Team? Well, overlaying the team member analysis (from earlier in this section), the CEO sees just two members of the team in the Peak Zone. They are Grace and (perhaps not surprisingly the CEO himself).

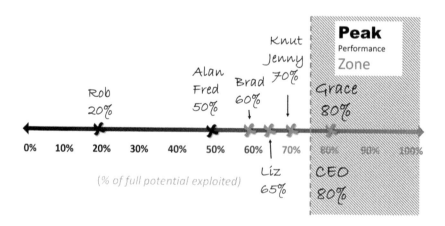

Senior Leadership Team Profile
% Full Potential Exploited - Jan. 2018

To have just two peak performers on a team of eight people is not unusual. Indeed, as we will see peak performance is not the norm. Consistent with other teams, most people on this leadership team are to be found within 10 percentage points of 65%. This is what we call the Normal Zone.

The Normal Zone

When it comes to performance the norm is between 55% and 74%. That is why it is called the Zone of Normal. The result is an 'everyday' or 'business-as-usual' level of performance. From the leadership team example on the previous page there are 4 people in this zone (i.e. Knut, Jenny, Liz and Brad). Their performance is predictable and reliable, but it won't 'set the world on fire'.

The Zone of Normal is a relatively safe place to be, surrounded on either side by danger - the risks associated with under-performance, as well as peak performance (e.g. burnout). It could also be called the Comfort Zone - comfortable for all except high performers. This is the territory of the salon car - it is reliable, steady and comfortable. For more glamor or acceleration look elsewhere.

'Everybody will tell you they are interested in performance', says one member of the pitstop partner community, but he adds 'in most cases it is just lip service'. In his words '**it is performance with a small 'p', rather than a capital 'P''**. 'They are not prepared to stretch beyond the comfort zone - to 'push the envelope', or 'rock the boat' he adds. In many cases the organization or team environment won't reward it, it may not even allow it.

Danger Zone

Where the P2P Metric™ falls below 55% an alarm bell should go off - warning the leader that something is seriously wrong and alerting him or her to danger. Below 55% is what we call the 'Zone of Danger' with three of the eight members of the senior leadership team in our earlier example to be found there.

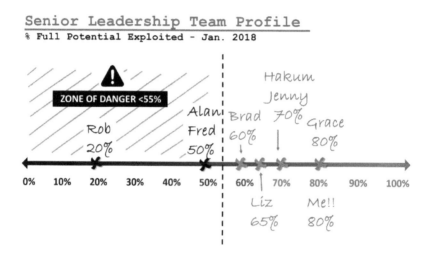

Being in the 'Danger Zone' (26%-55%) is damaging to the well-being of the individual, as well as the team. It can result in a downward spiral of confidence and motivation, as well as tension with the leader and conflict within the team. Those in the zone are likely to be disengaged and may be at risk of leaving. Furthermore, there is the risk of contagion outside the zone with poor performance and its associated behaviors often spreading throughout the group or team[27].

Crisis Zone

The deeper a person is into the 'Danger Zone', the greater the cause for concern.   In the above example Rob is operating at a jaw-dropping 20% of his full potential. That puts him in the 'Crisis Zone' (i.e. <25%) with acute implications not just for Rob's performance, but for his well-being too.[28] The result is a crisis of confidence and motivation. Importantly, there are likely to be consequences for the entire team, with many eyes focused on how the situation is handled (if at all).

Here is a diagram to help you recap on the 4 Zones of Performance.

Zones of Performance

Crisis	Danger Zone	NORMAL Zone	Peak Performance Zone
<25%	<55%	55-74%	75+%

0%   10%   20%   30%   40%   50%   60%   70%   80%   90%   100%
(% of full potential exploited)

There is a larger version of this visual at the end of the section for use in profiling the members of your team.

FORWARD THINKING

Continuing the senior leadership team example from earlier, the CEO's ambition is to take the team from performing at 60% to 80% of its potential (shown below).

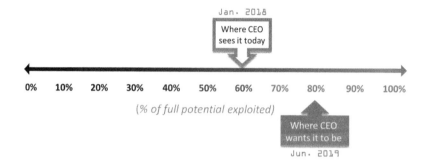

What is the performance goal for your organization or team? To find out complete the following steps with your team:

- Give each person a copy of the panels overleaf

- Ask people to first complete the page privately (5 mins).

- When complete each person has 3 mins to share with the group.

- Pool all the answers together and discuss as a team.

When the exercise is complete, read the remainder of this section to see if your team has passed or failed the BIG question test.

1 **TODAY**

Show (on the scale) the % of your team's full potential exploited **today**. Use the panel (below) to explain why.

The BIG Question

2 **24 MONTHS**

Show (on the scale) where you want your team to be **in 24 months**. Use the panel (below) to explain the difference.

0%   10%   20%   30%   40%   50%   60%   70%   80%   90%   100%

(% of full potential exploited)

TODAY in brief

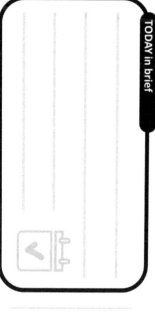

In Brief: 24 MONTHS

3 How important is this improvement to you?

1   2   3   4   5
Score: 1=Not Important at all, 5 = Very Important

4 How confident are you that it can be achieved?

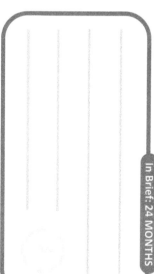

1   2   3   4   5
Score: 1=Not Important at all, 5 = Very Important

IT'S A TEST – A BIG TEST!

How a unit or team talks about the BIG question and, what, if anything, it does when it stops talking is a test. Find out what it reveals about your team by answering the questions overleaf.

(a) Your Team's Performance Mindset

The BIG performance question is a gauge of the level of interest in the issue of performance – as reflected in the level of energy and engagement that results[29]. For example, the question should get a person to pause and reflect. If a person answers abruptly and then says 'next question please...' that reveals a lot about their desire or ability to engage in a dialog about performance. If a person, or a team cannot get energized or exercised about their own potential they have failed the first test.

The 4 Tests: What does the BIG question reveal about your organization/team's approach to performance? Find out by answering the questions bellow:

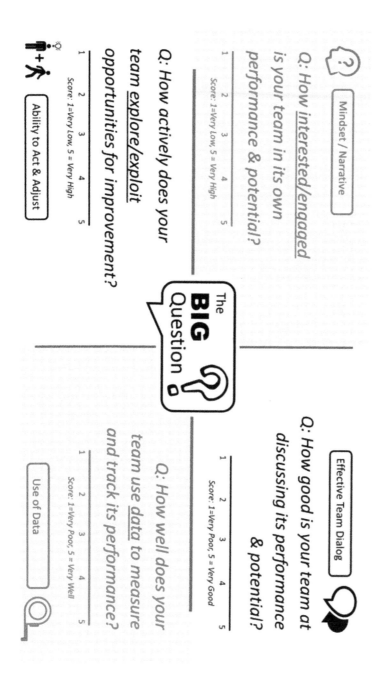

Mindset / Narrative

Q: How interested/engaged is your team in its own performance & potential?

1   2   3   4   5
Score: 1=Very Low, 5 = Very High

Effective Team Dialog

Q: How good is your team at discussing its performance & potential?

1   2   3   4   5
Score: 1=Very Poor, 5 = Very Good

The BIG Question

Q: How actively does your team explore/exploit opportunities for improvement?

1   2   3   4   5
Score: 1=Very Low, 5 = Very High

Ability to Act & Adjust

Q: How well does your team use data to measure and track its performance?

1   2   3   4   5
Score: 1=Very Poor, 5 = Very Well

Use of Data

(b) Your Team's Ability to Dialog Performance

One characteristic of peak performing managers and their teams should come as little surprise - they think about performance - a lot. Moreover, they talk about it in a way that is open and honest, because it is safe to do so[30]. What happens in your organization or team? Talking about performance may not be easy, but it is easy to put off. When the conversation does happen, politics and personalities can creep in, followed by defensiveness and blame.

An effective dialog about performance or potential won't always be comfortable or pleasant. Indeed, moving the dial on performance requires that some tension is present. That was clear in a recent pitstop workshop where the CEO put performance at 75% while some department heads give answers as low as 45%. The BIG performance question is not a test of whether people can agree, but whether they **can disagree and still have an effective dialog[31]**.

(c) Your Team's Ability to Act & Adjust

The ability to talk about performance is important, but it is not enough. That is unless the talk is put into action and those involved are prepared to renew their efforts and modify/adapt their approach. Be warned however: If people display a low level of energy and engagement when they are talking about performance, then it would be foolish to expect anything different when it comes to implementation or change.

Look at the wording of the BIG question. Although the question is about performance, it is the word 'potential' that is actually used. This is deliberate - the objective is to ensure **a future-focused and positive** debate that engages and energizes all those involved.

(d) Your Team's Ability to Measure Performance

There are two ways of answering the BIG question – one involves gut instinct and the other involves measurement and data. The leader's direct first-hand experience of working with a team is important and can be very insightful. However, there are things that one cannot see. It is vital to bring objective analysis and external benchmarking to any questions regarding performance. The BIG performance question is a test of whether there is clear agreement about how performance should be measured, as well as verifiable data to back it up.

BIG Data and Your P2P Metric™

The BIG question requires BIG data. Inspired by the use of BIG data to drive performance in F1™, the PitStop Analytics™ platform scientifically measures performance and potential within organizations, business units, teams, and individuals. It calculates the performance potential (P2P Metric™) based on 186 performance parameters and variables. It **systematically scans for performance losses, risks and gains** – measuring, categorizing, and prioritizing them. Data gathering is cloud-based and takes just 26 mins per person. Then algorithms and predictive models take over.

WHAT'S NEXT?

In this section you will have estimated the performance potential of your organization, business unit or team – that is its P2P Metric™. This means you can plot your team's Zone of Performance. So, before you move on, take a moment to position yourself and your unit or team on the diagram overleaf.

In the next section we will seek to make sense of all of this - exploring the reasons why your team is where it is at and what can be done to move into (or if you are there already, to stay within) the Zone of Peak Performance™.

Apply the BIG question to position yourself and your unit or team on across the various zones below:

(% of full potential exploited)

SECTION 2

PERFORMANCE LOSSES & GAINS

INTRODUCTION

In the last section we mapped your unit or team to a particular Zone of Performance, based on the BIG question and P2P Metric™. Now it is time to understand why your unit or team is where it is and the factors that will either keep it there, or move it elsewhere.

The objective of this section is to identify the barriers as well as the risks to peak performance within your organization, or team. First, we will use the traditional approach, but on recognizing its limitations, we will introduce the concept of Performance Losses and Gains as a more scientific and robust means of realizing and sustaining peak performance.

INTRODUCING THE 'NEW' NORMAL

We have asked the BIG question of thousands of leaders across 47 markets and 13 industries. The average of all the answers is a P2P Score of just 61%[32]. In other words, **organizations, business units and teams are on average performing at just 61% of their full potential**[33]. Some are higher and some are lower, but a statistical graph of the standard deviation clearly suggests a new normal. That normal is the 61% standard for performance[34].

Does the average P2P Metric™ of 61% surprise you? Maybe you are thinking it is a long way from F1™ levels of performance. Well, there are two ways to view the data.

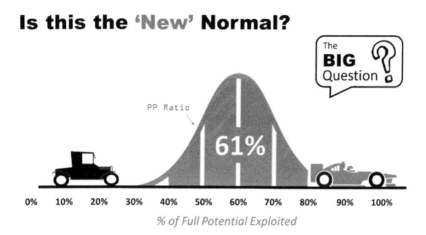

BETWEEN TWO MINDS

We find ourselves between two minds when it comes to the data about performance (i.e. the 61%). We flit between 'glass half-empty' and 'glass half-full' all the time – although the glass is more an oilcan if you follow the racing metaphor of this book.

When the glass or oilcan is half-empty we say that **61% is neither normal or acceptable**. Operating at less than two-thirds may be the norm, but it is a very strange kind of normal! Imagine your plant or facility was running at a mere 61% of its capacity - it would be a major call to action. However, we are not just talking about factories, buildings or machines operating at just 61%, but entire organizations, business units and teams. Such a figure represents a major drain not just on performance, but on talent, energy and innovation too. It is not excellence! ...it is not thriving! ...and it is not winning either! Moreover, there is a price to be paid for this under-performance – by workers, customers, shareholders and even societies.

Oilcan is half-full
POTENTIAL:
39% = BIG
Opportunity!

Oilcan is half-empty
PERFORMANCE:
61% = BIG
Disappointment!

The **BIG** Question

When the 'can is half-full' and we are seeing the positive, the unexploited 39% represents a big opportunity for leaders - perhaps the biggest of all opportunities. **Exploiting even a small proportion of so much unused potential could transform organizations and teams, as well as economies**. Just think of the new ideas, products and innovations that would result! Everybody would benefit – shareholders, customers and, of course, leaders and their teams. The dividend would be improved wellbeing[35], as well as better performance.[36] The result - more meaningful work and more satisfied, even healthier workers.

Pause for a moment to imagine your team performing at 80%, 90% or even 95% - what possibilities would that create for you, your team, the organization and even the broader society[37]?

_____

_____

_____

Mindset is critical to performance, but regardless of whether the glass/can is half-full or half-empty, the challenge is the same – how to unlock the potential of organizations, teams and individuals? **It is all academic, unless we can find new and better ways to unlock the potential for performance.** This has been the guiding motivation for this book and the extensive program of research behind it.

NO SHORTAGE OF POTENTIAL!

When it comes to performance the problem is not a shortage of potential. That deserves to be written in BIG letters because it has profound implications – especially for the many leaders who have been struggling with traditional performance management[38], or even leadership development and team-building.

It deserves to be in BIG Letters..

The problem is **not** that the potential does not exist, but that organizations and their leaders have struggled to **deliberately, systematically and creatively unlock individual and collective potential** within their organizations, business units and teams. Most important of all they have failed to systematically identify, tackle and remove the obstacles to individuals and teams realizing 75%, 85% or even 90% of their potential. It is not even clear who is responsible for it[39]. Moreover, it does not help that potential can be fuzzy and hard to measure[40], that it defies short term solutions, or that a multidisciplinary approach is required[41].

UNLOCKING THE POTENTIAL

There are many reasons why organizations, business units and teams leave so much potential unexploited. There are situational and structural factors, including culture, leadership, environment and strategy. There are also issues of skills, attitudes and behaviors. Indeed, there are almost 200 factors in total[42].

Unless we understand and engage with these factors we won't be able to do much to drive future performance. Given the tools, even the language, presently available to managers that can be a challenge. For example: **How easy would it be to get agreement as to the factors preventing your team from realizing its full potential?** Well, let's use the diagram overleaf to find out – fill it out yourself but before you do copy the page for some of your colleagues to answer also. When everybody is finished ask them to share and then set your watch to see how long it takes to get agreement on the top 3.

You are likely to end up with a long list of factors preventing your team realizing its full potential. But how comprehensive or scientific is the list? Some of the factors identified may be overlapping, while others may have been overlooked. Chances are the answers will vary widely, so too will the language used to describe them.

Different people, depending on their background and role, are likely to have their own perspectives on which of the factors are most important. Expect that there will be some politics involved and some personality issues too. The debate might even get heated, with some of the contributions seen as either excuses or accusations.

All of the above goes to show that there is **no standardized or efficient way of identifying the causes of under-performance** within an organization, business unit or team[43]. But if identifying these factors is difficult, tackling them is going to be more difficult still.

What is **preventing** your team from
realizing its full potential?

Please list 3-5 key factors below:

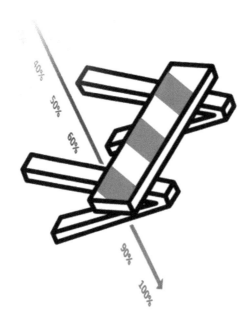

If only there was a way to make it easier. That is a scientific model or data-driven process for identifying and exploiting an organization or team's unexploited potential. It is this unmet need that the Pitstop Meta-model™ (introduced in the next section) and the analytics solution behind it, has been designed to meet.

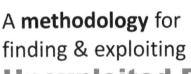

A **methodology** for finding & exploiting **Unexploited Potential**

This book is the culmination of a decade of research into the unexploited potential of teams and how it can be unlocked. Starting in the next chapter we will begin to build a new model and process to systematically find and exploit the next 5%, 10%, 15% or more of your team's performance potential. But first we are going to equip you with a new language and construct for the task.

Barriers to Performance

Here are the barriers to performance most commonly identified by leaders and their teams. But how accurate or scientific is the list? For example: Can you spot anything missing?

Most Common Barriers

1. Clarity on Results

2. Poor Communication

3. Poor Accountability

4. Lack of Discipline

5. Poor Sense of Urgency

6. Clarity of Roles & Responsibilities

7. Lack of Alignment

8. Lack of Focus

9. Slow to change

10. Low trust

But, what's missing from the list?

Pitstop research has identified a total of 186 potential barriers to the performance of business units and teams. The PitStop Analytics™ platform **systematically scans** for these factors using BIG data analytics and visualization techniques (see appendix).

PERFORMANCE LOSSES

Behind the BIG question (in the last section) there is a BIG idea and a small (but important) piece of mathematics. It is called Performance Losses (or alternatively gains) and is our starting point in the exploration of why organizations and teams fail to exploit so much of their potential.

It has been long known that there are inherent inefficiencies in the process of people working together. Called 'Process Losses' these help to explain why so many organizations and teams fail to live up to their promise[44]. The concept of process losses is very important, but somewhat esoteric. To engage managers, we replace the word 'Process' with 'Performance' and talk, not just about losses, but gains too.

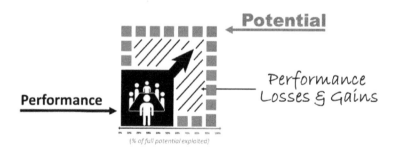

Process Losses describe how the output and efficiency of a group or team can be diminished by the behaviors and interactions of its members. These are important in explaining why teams fail to realize their full potential. However, there are other factors too, such as structures, process, leadership, strategy and execution. It is the totality of all these factors that we describe as 'Performance Losses'. Technically speaking, these are **the difference between the performance and the potential of an organization, team or individual**. In other words, the gap between the actual output or effectiveness of an organization / team and what it is capable of.

Performance Losses are the reason why your team has not yet realized its full potential. They are the difference between where your team is today and where you want it to be in the future – the reason why it is at 55% or 65% and not 75% or 85% for example.

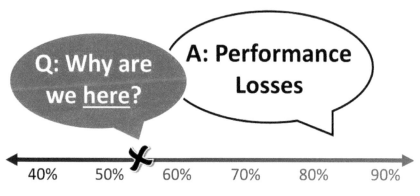

(% full potential exploited)

Because many performance losses are cultural, structural or systemic they can be slow to change. So, not only do they explain where your team is today, but they threaten to keep it there. That is the bad news, but there is good news too. For every Performance Loss there is an equal, if not greater, Performance Gain. If deliberately tackled, Performance Losses offer the prospect of future Performance Gains – the next 5%, 10% or 20% that could take your team into the Zone of Peak Performance™ (as discussed in Section 1).

Neutral Language - Positive Debate

The language of performance losses and gains is deliberately neutral. It is a non-judgmental matter-of-fact terminology, consistent with scientific measurement and objective analysis. This is to overcome the challenges associated with traditional Performance Management[45] and enable people to talk openly and honestly about performance[46]. Performance Losses are neither excuses nor accusations. The objective is to depersonalize and depoliticize the issue of performance. It is also to encourage 'systems thinking' – to look beyond people or events to the systemic or underlying causes of under-performance[47].

CALCULATING LOSSES / GAINS

What gets measured gets managed, so it is important to put a number around performance losses and potential gains. Although it takes an algorithm to do this scientifically[48], the principle involved can be demonstrated quite simply. In the panel below enter the % of your org/team's full potential exploited (the answer to the BIG question in Section 1) and subtract it from 100%. Write the answer in the panel below:

Insert % potential exploited here

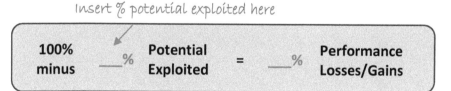

As you will recall, teams in our research say they are realizing 61% of their potential. That puts the average figure for performance losses or gains at 39% (i.e. 100% - 61% = 39%). That 39%, or the equivalent figure for your organization/team, is something to get excited about.

Performance Gains/Losses

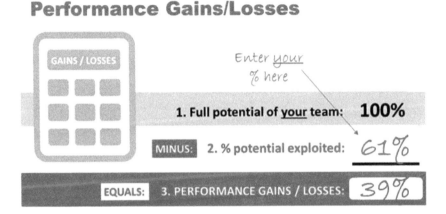

Of course, not all of the 100% shown above is available to an organization, business unit or team. You will recall from Section 1 that we defined the Zone of Peak Performance™ as 75% plus. So, with realism and sustainability in mind you might like to adjust your calculation accordingly.

> What are Performance Losses and Gains? How do I identify them? ...and most importantly how can I transform them into gains? That's what the remainder of this book is all about. Specifically, the objective is to enable your team to identify and exploit the next 5%, 15% or 25% of its potential using a systematic meta model and process.

Performance on the Racetrack

Spoiler alert! In the next section will introduce the F1™-inspired Pitstop Meta-model™ which identifies the most common performance losses within organizations and teams under 22 headings, based on an analysis of 186 performance-related variables. At the highest level these performance losses and potential gains can be grouped in line with the following racing equation:

I believe that pure speed isn't always the point; it's what you manage to get out of your potential. And that's where I've always been very successful. You know, really working deep with the team, maximizing my possibilities.
Michael Schumacher[49]

LOSSES OR GAINS

We are often asked about the dichotomy between Performance Losses and Gains. For example: Are they the same thing? Well, to explain we will turn to a motivational speaker and a behavioral economist. One will make the case for talking about Performance Losses, the other will make the case for Performance Gains.

(a) Performance Gains

Performance Gains is about hope and aspiration. It is a positive psychology 'be all you can be' message – the kind you might hear from a motivational speaker such as Tony Robbins or Zig Ziglar:

MESSAGE: **A**

Imagine your team realizing its full potential...

Delivering a **greater performance** for the organization while also **bringing out the best** in its people....

A **great place to work** where passion talent & people **thrive'**.

Team Performance is not fixed. There is no more positive or encouraging message than that. Your team may be operating at 55% or 65% of its full potential today, but it is not stuck there.

(b) Performance Losses

Daniel Kahneman is the Nobel Prize winning father of Behavioral Economics. Kahneman no doubt believes in potential but after decades of research he also knows that **our decisions are skewed more towards the prevention of loss** rather than the exploitation of gains[50]. He also knows that we are biased towards the short term, rather than the long term. That would put him firmly in the

Performance Losses camp, with a message such as that labelled B below.

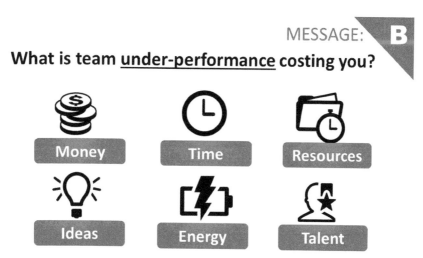

The Performance Losses message is one of underperformance, inefficiency and waste. The company is paying wages and people are doing their work, but to have them performing at 55% or 65% of their full potential is a waste of time, money and resources, as well as talent, energy and ideas. Just as tackling waste and inefficiency in other areas of business is essential, so too is minimizing performance losses within teams. Given that people are one of the biggest overheads in any business, the zeal for reducing performance losses should be as great as (if not greater than) that for cutting costs in IT, operations or any other area.

Performance losses exist in every organization or team. Like gravity they are a fundamental force of nature. They don't just affect others. At this very time there are performance losses acting on your team too. The question is: How actively is your organization, business unit or team working to tackle them?

While the term 'performance losses' appeals to managers with spreadsheets and calculators, the concept goes beyond numbers[51]. It is not just the organization that is losing, but its people too. Their natural energy and creativity is being suppressed by poor alignment, dysfunctional teams, bureaucratic processes and so on.

If your team is struggling, Performance Losses are the cause. They don't just affect the task effectiveness of your team, but also its ability to make good decisions, to learn or innovate[52]. The implications extend beyond performance to include your team's well-being and social health too[53]. The latter may sound soft and inconsequential, but in the context of realizing and sustaining peak levels of individual and collective performance they are essential[54].

GAINS OR LOSSES – YOUR CHOICE

Pause for a moment to re-read the two messages – marked A and B. Which one resonates most with you – gains (message A) or losses (message B)? Are you with the motivational speaker, or the behavioral economist? Mark your choice below.

Message A	Message B
☐	☐
You are motivated by:	You are motivated by:
Performance Gains	**Performance Losses**

The choice between A and B is a philosophical one. There is no right or wrong answer, it is just a matter of what best motivates you. What about us (in the Growth Pitstop™ Community)? Well, we like to focus on the positive and passionately believe in the potential of individuals and teams. So, we prefer Message A. However, we sometimes find that we are more passionate about the potential of teams than their managers. When this happens we dutifully switch from talking about performance gains to calculating performance losses. This generally adds extra urgency and adrenaline into the performance debate – such as overleaf.

> Whether you are taken by Performance Losses or Gains may reveal something about you. According to psychologists, people can be grouped according to the two dominant motivations[55]:
>
> - Motivation 1: **Not to lose** - If this is your dominant motivation then Performance Losses and Performance Risks are likely to appeal most to you.
>
> - Motivation 2: **To Win/Gain** - If this is your dominant motivation then Performance Gains are most likely to appeal to you.

PERFORMANCE GAINS

One member of the Growth Pitstop™ partner community has a powerful way of explaining the difference between performance losses and gains. For her it is more about intent than it is about language. As she puts it: 'performance losses become gains if you actively work to improve organization/team performance, but they are losses (and stay losses forever) if you sit by and do nothing'. The process of taking action is called transforming performance losses into gains.

Calculating the Cost

The HRD partner waited pen in hand while the tech company CEO did some mental arithmetic. The number was $4.1 million - that was the annual cost of the senior leadership team – the same team analyzed in Section 1. The CEO then went on to explain the math involved '...there are nine people on the senior leadership team, all have an attractive executive package and travel allowances, as well as corner offices and personal assistants'. 'All in, I'd say the cost figure of $4.1 million is a fairly good estimate' the CEO confirmed with a nod. That number was the final piece of information required to complete the analysis (shown below).

Calculating Process Losses

Senior Leadership Team = 9 people

% full potential exploited = 60%

Cost of team = $4.1m

Performance losses = $1.6m
(Estimate)

Suddenly the CEO's answer to the BIG question (i.e. 60%) took on a deeper significance. At a running cost of $4.1m, the team's performance losses could now be estimated at $1.6m[56].

What are your team's performance losses when calculated as a % of its annual running costs?

If you are wondering how to get from 61% to 75% (or anywhere else), then the answer is to transform process losses into gains.

Most performance losses can be transformed into gains, with time, effort and discipline. For those losses that cannot, there is the prospect of compensating gains to be found elsewhere. The performance gain can be big or small, direct or indirect, including:

- Increased output, quality or efficiency
- Improved top line or bottom line
- Reduced waste - time, money or resources saved
- Improved information and decision-making
- Enhanced creativity and innovation
- Improved social health or cohesion of a team
- More engagement - talent and energy unleashed.

Use the tick boxes above to identify the type of performance gains you believe can be realized for your organization, business unit, or team.

Performance Gains are all the losses identified earlier (time, money, talent, etc.), but in reverse. However, those measured in hours and days have special appeal for today's busy managers. As one project leader recently proclaimed during a pitstop; 'I truly believe that if we work together more effectively as a team each of us could save 2 to 3 hours per week'. The newly formed international project team of 26 had already gained a reputation for marathon conference calls, endless email chains and exhaustive CC lists. This was generating frustration and getting in the way of the team's work. 'Add up all those hours and it is the equivalent of two full team members!' exclaimed the leader. But the main motivation was self-serving. Performance losses often result in personal frustration and for this leader the challenges of team coordination had become a major stressor. The question is:

Q: How much time could you save if your team worked together more effectively?

PERFORMANCE RISKS

'What are the implications of your team operating at just 61% of its full potential?' asked a pitstop coach. The Division Head's response was an immediate one - '... it means that the team will struggle to deliver the results that are expected of it!". This illuminates a third category to add to Performance Losses and Gains, that is Performance Risks. Specifically, the risks posed to the achievement of target or delivery of key projects, priorities or strategies by the under-performance of any team.

Performance Risks

Can a team deliver 100% of its targeted results if it is operating at just 61% of its potential? In this age of stretch-targets the answer is more than likely 'no'.   That is why we always follow up the BIG question by asking about the level of confidence regarding the results or targets that an organization or team must achieve:

Q: How confident are you that your org./team will achieve its target/realize its goals? (circle on the scale below)

1	2	3	4	5	6	7	8	9	10

Not Confident   Absolutely
At All   Certain

Performance Risk goes beyond the delivery of results, strategies and projects to sustaining performance more generally. They can, for example, slow responsiveness and innovation leaving the organization vulnerable to threats, or blind to opportunities. They can also increase other business risks, such as the loss of key talent and employee disengagement more generally.

BOUNDLESS POTENTIAL

The core message is that performance potential is not fixed. This applies equally to the potential of an organization, business or team. This is great news for those reaching a ceiling in terms of what is possible. That is why we use a dotted line to show that potential is flexible, rather than rigid – as in the diagram below.

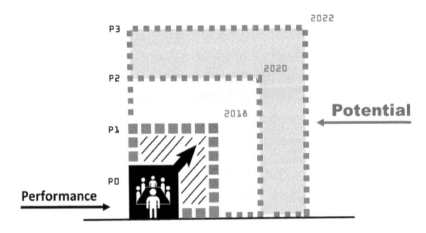

The dotted line for potential also hints that those factors that define the potential of an organization or team can be real or imagined. A unit or team's belief in its own potency and potential can have a major bearing on its level of performance57. Thus, building a sense of confidence and purpose can be as powerful as the more tangible measures aimed at extending the capacity of an organization or team.

The boundaries of capability and capacity can be shifted by internal and external events. Operating in the Zone of Peak Performance™ requires continually testing and indeed pushing the boundaries of what is possible. It means being on the lookout for game-changers, the next bounce of the ball[58] and new ways to jump the curve[59].

Q: What changes internal or external could significantly shift the boundaries of capacity & capability for your organisation or team?

WHAT'S NEXT?

Before you move on to the next Section, take a moment to recap on the Top 3 performance losses, gains and risks for your business unit or team by completing the page overleaf.

In the next section we will switch from diagnosing to modelling and predicting performance, introducing the Pitstop Meta-model™ for identifying and measuring performance losses. This is the basis for a systematic and data-driven process to convert performance losses into gains of 7-25% within organizations, business units and teams.

List the Top 3 performance losses, gains and risks for your business unit or team:

Performance LOSSES

Performance GAINS

Performance RISKS

0%   10%   20%   30%   40%   50%   60%   70%   80%   90%   100%

SECTION 3:

A TALE OF TWO TEAMS

INTRODUCTION

In recent decades there has been an explosion in the science of teams and team performance. To synthesise and make accessible the main findings of all this research we are going to tell the story of two teams:

- **One team is at peak performance** – it is highly coordinated, efficient and cohesive. It has been carefully set up to ensure that the right people are in the right roles, doing the right work and so on. There are substantial performance gains, as opposed to losses for this team, as per Section 2.

- **The other team is under-performing.** It has been pulled together, with little attention to size, composition, or purpose. It is rife with conflict, unclear on its purpose and struggling to do its work effectively. In the language of Section 1, this team has a low ratio of performance to potential or P2P Metric™. It is performing well below its potential.

To paraphrase the classic Dicken's novel 'it was the best of teams, it was the worst of teams'[60]. The story of the two teams/organizations will bring to life the concepts of performance-potential and Zones of Performance (Section 1), as well as Performance Losses and Gains (Section 2). What makes it even more fascinating is that it is also a story of how the basis of competition can change in an industry, business or sport. The teams we will study belong to one of the most high-pressure and performance obsessed fields of human endeavor – the fastest track sport on earth; F1™. They tell the story of how the requirements of winning have shifted in recent decades.

NEW BASIS OF COMPETITION

In 1984, the formula for winning in F1™ was turned on its head. For the first time, stopping (or to be more precise pit stopping) during a race helped the driver to win. In a sport where milliseconds separate the winner from the rest, it was a fundamental shift in the basis of competition. F1™ had long been about fearless and somewhat egotistical drivers competing in a gladiatorial style battle on the track. Once the race started, success or failure was in the hands of the driver and the driver alone. Now, with the introduction of the pitstop, teams finally had a role to play in the driver's race performance. The sport went from being about a great driver and a great car, to include having a great pit team[61]. Today, this transition from champion driver to winning team is also underway within most organizations. The story of teams in F1™ offers inspiration for organizations where the basis of success is shifting from individual to collaborative.

Never think that success is down to your own performance alone... The flowers of victory belong in many vases.
Michael Schumacher[62]

Performance in business, as in F1™, is a complex equation of driver, team and machine (shown overleaf). The driver, well that is you! The car is the various projects, initiatives, strategies and priorities that you are driving. The pit team is the people you need to win. They keep your car on the road, monitor its progress and make important adjustments as needed.

Traditionally the focus has been on the driver or the car – that is the leader and the strategy of the organization. However, it is becoming increasingly evident that this focus represents a significant blind spot. According to data from such authoritative sources as Harvard[63] and McKinsey[64], this driver or car only view of performance misses out on as much as 50% of the success of an organization. A total view of performance must focus on all 3 elements of driver, machine and team. This is the total performance equation. The question is: Where will you focus?

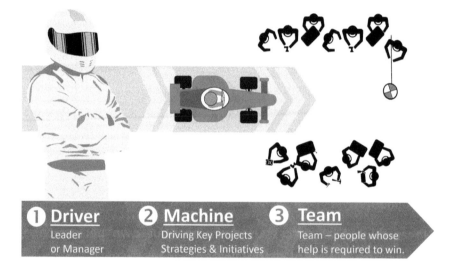

In the quest to identify performance losses and transform them into gains, organizations must continually work on all 3 factors in parallel; driver, machine and team. That is the key message at the core of the Pitstop Meta-model™ as shown overleaf. Built upon the principles of mental modelling and cognitive reframing[65], the meta-model explores performance in the context of a pitstop for the driver, machine and team.

The Pitstop Meta-Model™

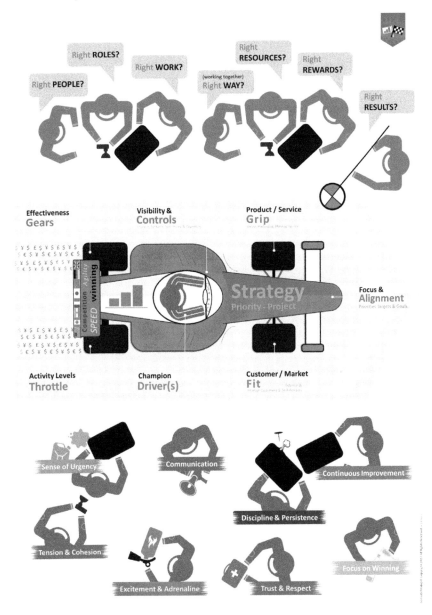

A NEW MODEL OF PERFORMANCE

The Pitstop Meta-model™ has intuitive appeal, particularly when compared to traditional business models with their straight lines and square boxes[66]. That appeal works regardless of functional background or language/culture. However, there is much complexity behind the visual clarity and simplicity of the meta-model. For example, while the model has 22 labels – corresponding to key performance parameters, it is built around 186 variables and a complex mathematical algorithm (this is the core of the Pitstop Analytics™ solution).

Pitstop Meta-model™ - in numbers:

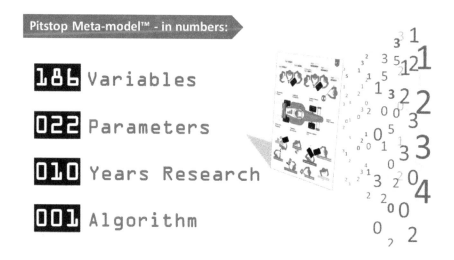

186 Variables

022 Parameters

010 Years Research

001 Algorithm

Why the Pitstop Meta-model™? Well, you cannot move your Performance Potential (P2P Metric™) from 60% to 70% or anything else, without actively working on the factors shown in the model. These are the key performance losses that can be transformed into measurable gains.

Use the model to
<u>MOVE</u> your org./team's:

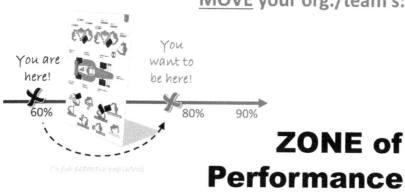

ZONE of
Performance

The single page view of the model has a total of 22 performance losses and gains organized into the top, middle and bottom of the model, however each of these factors has up to a dozen related and interdependent variables. That brings the total number of variables examined to 186. This means big data in the case of a large organization or team – an estimated 262,260 data points for an organization or team of 1000 people.

Use the model to
<u>FIND</u> your org./team's:

Performance
Losses & Gains

In this book, we will zoom in on parts of the model, that while often neglected, represent a major source of performance losses for many organizations. That is the complex subject of team performance (top and bottom of the meta-model). As evidence of the potential that exists in this area, let's return to the story of teams and the role of the pitstop in F1™.

> *A simple visual image is one of the best ways to help a group see the same thing at the same time. Many of the most influential ideas in the field of strategy have been expressed in memorable visual frameworks.*
> Chris Ertel & Lisa Kay Solomon[67]

PIT TEAM SCIENCE – A HISTORY

F1™ has pioneered many technologies that are today a standard feature of the everyday motor car[68]. But the sport's obsession with design and innovation doesn't stop there. It has also been rigorously applied to the performance of not just machines, but people too. This is immediately evident to anybody who looks into a pit lane during a championship race. As Sam Michael, former Sporting Director at McLaren Mercedes puts it; *'...the pitstop has... become like another car development area...'*[69] The sport has transformed teamwork from an art to a science. When it comes to team performance, F1™ started before the professors and consultants. Indeed, for almost four decades F1™ has been innovating its own laboratory of team performance – the pit lane.

> *Considering the millions of dollars spent on designing, manufacturing and developing a modern Formula One™ car... it's paradoxical that one of the most important parts of a Grand Prix comes when the car is stationary.*
> Mark Gallagher[70]

Today's F1™ pit teams are an inspiration. In just 2 seconds, 20 people surround the car, change all 4 tires and make any other adjustments required to maximize the driver's chances of winning. Now imagine your team working with the same focus, intensity and determination to win!

The choreographed precision of today's pit teams sets a new bar for team performance, but it hasn't always been that way. In the earlier years of racing, pit stops were clumsy and slow. In the 1950's and early 1960's drivers got out of their cars for a drink and a cigarette, as three people in overalls shuffled around the car with wrenches, hammers and an oil can. All this happened at the side of the track as cars whizzed by – dedicated pit lanes are a relatively new addition to racing. It is laughable by today's standards, but in those early days what happened in the pit lane didn't much matter. It was not connected with winning, indeed it was more likely to lose the race, than win it. On August 15, 1982, all that changed.

Aug. 1982:

The 1st Real

PITSTOP

It was mid-way through the Austrian Grand Prix. Brazilian driver Nelson Piquet had just pulled into the pitlane and the first pitstop of the modern era unfolded. Today, we have seen it a hundred times, the choreography of a pit team in action. But on that summer day in Austria, spectators looked on in amazement at the first planned mid-race fuel and tyre pitstop ever. It was a radical innovation that enabled Piquet and his team to win[71]. The brainchild of Brabham's Technical Director Gordon Murray, this extraordinary pitstop would have made Frederick Taylor, Henry Ford or Edward Deming smile[72]. There were clever tools, efficient processes, specialised work teams and of course a stopwatch! All the other F1™ teams quickly followed suit and that is how the pitstop became a model of team performance. More than 30 years later it still offers inspiration for teams.

PitStop Evolution: From Art to Science

Machine	Simple	Complex
Its involves:	3 Individuals	Team of 20+
Speed:	Minutes	Milliseconds
Measurement:	No Data	Big Data

How do you change the tyres quickly? How do you put the fuel in quickly...? We videoed the mechanics changing tyres, analysed it frame by frame, and I redesigned the hubs, bearing carriers, threads, nuts and wheel guns...
Gordon Murray, *father of the modern pitstop*[73]

LESSONS FOR ORGANIZATIONS

Race teams invest countless millions in building high performance racing machines – each year developing ever more sophisticated models. What is less well known is that they apply similar efforts in respect of team, and in particular pit team, performance. They have turned collaborative people performance into a science. By contrast, most organizations bring groups of people together and expect high levels of performance yet leave the rest to chance. Unlike Gordon Murray, they pay little attention to the roles, processes or tools that are required for high performance. They don't pay enough attention to issues of team size, composition, structure and process. That is why F1™ offers so many lessons for organizations that want to design teams capable of performing complex demanding work in high-pressure environments.

The precisely-timed, millimeter-perfect choreography of a modern pitstop is vital to help teams to turn their race strategy into success.
F1.com

When it comes to pit team performance in F1™ nothing is left to chance. The processes and tools are continually adapted and pit teams practice and train assiduously. For all those involved continuous improvement is not a byword, it is a relentless quest for the millisecond advantage. Now the science and sophistication applied to pit teams since the 1980s, can be applied to teams in business and elsewhere. Are you ready to apply it to your team?

In the pages that follow, we combine inspiration from F1™ with Growth Pitstop™ research and analytics on 900 business teams and the latest findings from leading academic institutions and consulting houses.

A TALE OF TWO TEAMS

The meta-model is a tale of two teams. The top of the meta-model shows the peak performing 'dream team', with the dysfunctional rag-tag team at the bottom.

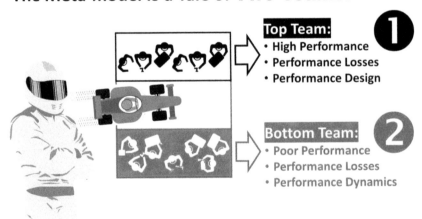

The Meta-model is a Tale of Two Teams:

Top Team:
• High Performance
• Performance Losses
• Performance Design
①

Bottom Team:
• Poor Performance
• Performance Losses
• Performance Dynamics
②

As we said a little earlier, the car at the centre of the performance meta-model represents the various projects, initiatives, strategies or priorities that you are driving. Your pit team is the people who must keep them on the road, monitor their progress and make any adjustments required for success. If your team is like that at the top of the model (i.e. peak performing) then the chances of winning are high. On the other hand, if your team is struggling and dysfunctional (like that at the bottom of the model) success may be a long way off.

If the top of the meta-model is the ideal, then the bottom is closer to the reality of teamwork. Most teams can find themselves somewhere between the two. Let's explore where your team is, starting first with the top of the meta-model and then moving to the bottom.

TOP OF THE META-MODEL

Look at the top of the meta-model (shown below). There are high levels of symmetry, co-ordination and interdependence. The right people are in the right roles and they have the right tools too. It just looks right.

High-Performing Team
Max. Performance Gains

Each team member has their own role, yet they are completely interdependent. One person has the wheel gun, one person takes off the wheel and another puts it on. This happens at all four wheels. No matter how great the individual contribution of any team member is, the team cannot win unless everybody does their job well. Performance is a shared responsibility for all team members and all share the same definition of winning – to complete the fastest pitstop, so as to safely release the car and driver back into the race with the maximum chances of winning.

It is the high level of interdependence and mutual accountability that qualifies the pit team to be designated a 'real team'[74]. This is a team that exhibits the performance gains associated with effective teamwork. We would naturally expect performance losses to be minimal. But it is not an accident, this has been achieved by design.

> *All of F1™ is about teamwork - it is not about an individual sport anymore. A typical grand prix team is about 650 people and those people work on multitude of different aspects of the car.*
> Sam Michael, *Fmr. Director, McLaren Mercedes*[75]

Pitstops have evolved from slapdash chaos to precisely-timed perfection[76]. A great pitstop involves the right people in the right roles, doing the right work, working together in the right way, with the right resources and, most important of all, focused on the right results.   That is a lot to get right, as we will explore in Section 4:   Design for Performance.   It does not happen by accident. Building and maintaining a peak performing team is not easy. Indeed, it will require a lot of hard-work and discipline from all those involved, as well as a degree of emotional intelligence and self-monitoring.

The top of the meta-model shows real teamwork in action. It is what all teams should aspire to. But just as there are not that many pit teams, there are not that many peak performing teams either. That leads us to the bottom of the meta-model. The other end of the team performance spectrum.

> *'Many people wish that their corporate team could operate at the level of F1™… Now they can…*
> Derek Daly[77]

BOTTOM OF THE MODEL

The bottom of the meta-model contrasts with the peak performing team at the top. It is a team in name only – a pseudo team. This is a group of individuals, where everybody does their own thing. People are pointing in every which way, chaos and confusion are the inevitable consequences.

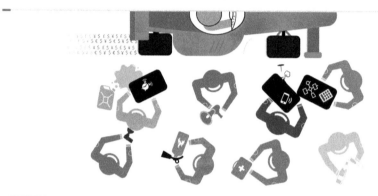

Max. Process <u>Losses</u>
Poor-Performing Team

These people are 'co-acting' in the same space, but exhibit independence, rather than interdependence[78]. The behaviors on display are not conducive to effective teamwork. There is competition rather than collaboration, with poor co-ordination and communication. Waste, conflict, fire-fighting and even sabotage are evident. The extent of performance losses within this team calls into question its very existence because all too often 'bad collaboration is worse than no collaboration at all'[79]. The team isn't winning, neither are the people on it. This is a team in name only - a pseudo team[80]. Instead it is acting like a crowd or a group.

Traditionally everything from a committee to a working group was classified as a 'team'. But the types of teams shown in the diagram are not all the same. They vary in size, structure and purpose. Most important of all, they vary in terms of performance. Under a new classification system, many of what we have traditionally called teams would be called something else; a 'Crowd', a 'Group', or a 'Team'[81].

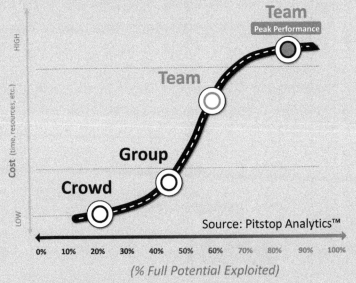

Rather than simply calling every unit of collaboration a 'team', people working collaboratively are to be found at different stages of the journey to peak performance (shown above). However, few will make it up hill and fewer still will be able to stay there for long without a continued focus on design and dynamics – that is the top and the bottom of the pitstop meta-model.

> 'Why is it that people spend so much time playing or working in groups that are not productive, effective, or cohesive?'
> Gordon Curphy & Robert Hogan[82]

WHERE TO NEXT?

Pit teams make their work look easy, but it is not. In racing as in business, effective teamwork requires:

- **Performance Design** - ensuring that the right people are in the right roles, doing the right work and so on. This is the top of the Pitstop to Perform model and is the subject of Part 1.

- **Performance Dynamics** - fostering the attitudes and behaviors that are required for effective collaboration. This is the bottom of the model and the subject of Part 2.

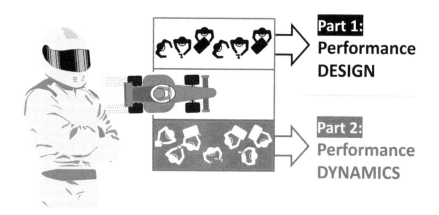

You cannot create real teams by convening a set of people and calling them a team. Instead, it takes careful thought and planning about the work the team will do, its composition, and the way it will be launched and developed.

Ruth Wageman, Debra A. Nunes, et al.[83]

As we will explore in the remainder of this book, Design and Dynamics represent two major sources of Performance Losses within organizations and teams. Transforming losses into gains in either of these areas offers the potential of moving your organization or team in the direction of peak performance.

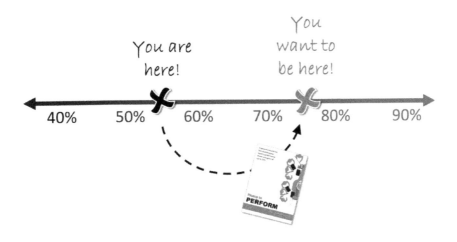

In the next section we will examine the working on Design (at the top of the meta-model) can move your organization or team.

Part 1:

PEAK PERFORMANCE

Exploring the top of the model, including:

- The structural characteristics of peak performance
- 7 Key design-related performance losses and gains
- How to design/ set-up teams for peak performance
- Right people in the right role, doing the right work, etc.

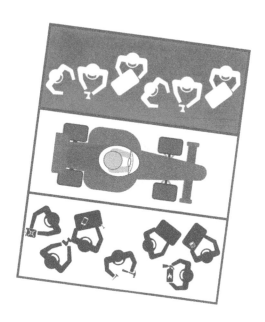

SECTION 3:

DESIGN FOR PERFORMANCE

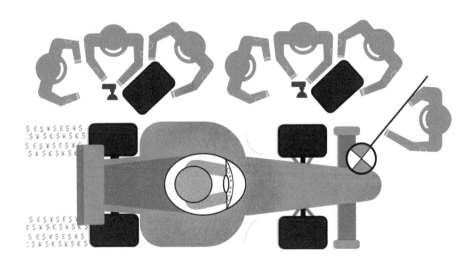

INTRODUCTION

A high performing organization or team is a beauty to behold - just watch a pit team in operation on race day. Such precisely choreographed teamwork, despite the pressures involved, is nothing short of inspirational. But what most people don't see (and what the race cameras don't show) is the amount of planning and preparation that goes into achieving and sustaining such a level of performance.

High-performing groups or teams do not naturally occur. They are not accidental either. Whether it is at the racetrack or in the executive suite, bringing a group of intelligent and experienced people together does not make for an effective team. Indeed, far from it. The performance of a pit team, or indeed any team, depends on getting a lot of things right. Indeed, at least 7 things as shown at the top of the meta-model. These are:

- RIGHT PEOPLE

- In the RIGHT ROLES

- Doing the RIGHT WORK

- Working together in the RIGHT WAY

- With the RIGHT RESOURCES

- And the RIGHT REWARDS

- To achieve the RIGHT RESULTS.

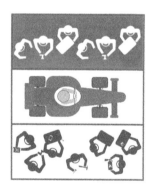

At first glance, this may seem like a straight-forward formula, however, when it comes to teams, 'getting it right' isn't easy. Indeed, teams as often get it wrong as right. When assessed against the 7 factors listed above, most groups or teams are simply not set-up for success.

Most teams are designed to fail rather than succeed. Quite simply, they don't have the right people in the right roles doing the right work and if they do, they are not working together in the right way, with the right resources, or towards the right results. If these things are wrong, rather than right, significant performance losses are to be expected. Most likely the team will only perform to the **standard of a group, or a crowd**. It certainly won't achieve the results of a peak performing team. To expect otherwise would be foolish, yet this is happening every day within organisations. It is this mismatch of expectations and results that has given many teams (and teamwork more generally) such a bad name.

> *It is difficult to get it right. …everybody has to do the perfect job to do the perfect pitstop, obviously!*
> John Carrey, Lotus Race Team Pit Crew[84]

PERFORMANCE BY DESIGN

Decades of research into peak performance presents both good and bad news. The bad news is that managers cannot make their groups and teams perform. However, the good news is that they are far from helpless. Managers can set their teams up for success by getting the design right. That means ensuring that the right people are in the right roles, working in the right way and so on. Team performance is a matter of **design rather than control**.

We design buildings, machines and products. We plan projects, budgets and even holidays. But when it comes to teams we do little of either. It is as if teams did not need to be planned or designed. It is this failure to plan for, or design, teams that is at the root of so much frustration and underperformance with respect to teamwork.

Most teams evolve with little thought and planning. Some are planned carefully at the start, but are slow to adjust and adapt to reflect changes in; the nature of work it must do, the environment in which it operates, or the stage of the team's own lifecycle. For most managers the concept of designing a team for performance is revolutionary and new.

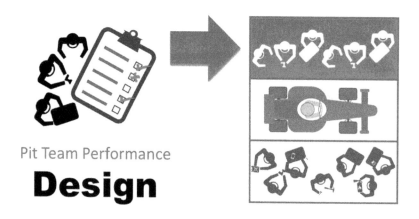

Pit Team Performance
Design

Team design requires quite a radical departure from the traditional approach adopted by managers. It also requires the abandonment of some fundamental (and fundamentally mistaken) beliefs about team performance. Principal among these is the belief that putting a team of good people together is enough to create a team.

> *No leader can make a team perform well. But all leaders can create conditions that increase the likelihood that it will.*
> J. Richard Hackman[85]

Managers carefully hire or select people (often at considerable cost) to join a team. Chosen, based on their past achievements as individuals, they are put working with other similarly talented people. What happens next? Well, in most cases that is left to chance! The expectation is that if the 'right people' are selected they will naturally perform as a team. More often than not the result is disappointment for all involved.

There is more to performance than simply bringing a group of capable individuals together and calling them a team[86]. That is a point that can't be repeated often enough. Even if you get the right people on the team, that is only one of a total of seven considerations in designing for team performance. Those people must be in the right roles, doing the right work and working towards the achievement of the right results. That is what team performance design is all about.

> *You cannot create real teams by convening a set of people and calling them a team. Instead, it takes careful thought and planning about the work the team will do, its composition, and the way it will be launched and developed.*
> Ruth Wageman, Debra A. Nunes, et al.[87]

PUTTING DESIGN FIRST

Organizations have long invested in team-building events and games, but not surprisingly struggle to quantify the return on investment on these activities. The new science of team performance and design explains why. The reality is that traditional team building and training while useful, will inevitably struggle in the face of flaws in team design. They can't tackle structural performance losses. Hence the message for managers is: **design comes first and team building second**.

Team
Design 1st

Team
Building 2nd

It is the leader or manager's job to ensure that the right people are in the right roles, that the team has the right purpose and so on. This is a surprise for those managers who have traditionally focused on team-building or managing interpersonal relations within teams. Team games, social nights or training programs have a role to play, but they cannot be expected to fix design-related problems, such as the wrong people in the wrong roles, or the lack of a clear and compelling purpose for the team. That requires working on team purpose, structure, process and so on. Just like building a house you need to start with the design first.

> *Sometimes the reason for the failure is that the team spent too much of its time in a group kumbaya and not enough on the task at hand.*
> Rich Karlgaard & Michael S. Malone[88]

SET-UP FOR SUCCESS

Is your organization or team set-up for performance and success? To find out answer the 7 questions below:

	Absolutely Disagree = 1, Absolutely Agree = 5
1. Do you have the **right people**?	1 2 3 4 5
2. Are those people in the **right roles**?	1 2 3 4 5
3. Are they doing the **right work**?	1 2 3 4 5
4. Are they working together in the **right way**?	1 2 3 4 5
5. Have they got the **right resources** (information, tools, etc.)?	1 2 3 4 5
6. Are they motivated with the **right rewards/incentives**?	1 2 3 4 5
7. Is the team focused on /delivering **the right results**?	1 2 3 4 5

The above questions are a powerful summary of a large tract of the research into organizational/team performance - what we label the 'design school'[89]. Let's add up your team's design score:

Score	What it means:
28-35:	Your team is set up for success. As a manager, your role is to 'coach' the team for success.
22-27:	A lot of the basics are in place to enable your team to perform, however keep working on improving the 7 factors to enable even higher levels of performance.

15-21:	Factors rated '1' or '2' represent performance losses for your team. Until they are tackled it will difficult to boost the performance.
<15:	Your team's design is seriously flawed and must inevitably represent a significant barrier to the creation of a cohesive or peak performing team.

If some of the essential 7 design factors are missing, your organization/team's performance will inevitably suffer. Moreover, your attempts at driving performance are likely to fail until they are addressed. The message for managers of underperforming teams is **change your expectations** regarding performance or alternatively change the design.

The Reality of Teams

The 7 design factors are interconnected. That is why design issues tend to come in twos, or threes. Indeed, 3 is the average from our analytics / research, or as one of our partner colleagues puts it 'you get three (design issues) for the price of one'. That means either there is an outright problem, or at least confusion / uncertainty with 3 design factors. Little wonder then that most teams underperform. Although this is a worrying finding, it is not all bad news. If managers work on the basics of their team's design, improved performance is almost inevitable.

Because of the frequency of design issues within teams, we say that the top of the model isn't normal. It is not natural for a group of people to come together and to work in such a closely coordinated manner. It is extraordinary, rather than ordinary - the result of careful stewardship as well as design. Moreover, it is the result of the wholehearted commitment of all involved.

The 7 Performance Design factors are shown visually here. Reflect on the factors shown for a few moments. How would you rank them in order of importance for your team?

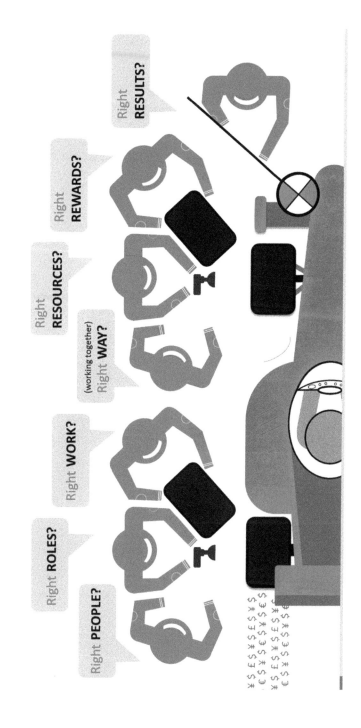

GETTING IT RIGHT

Any of the 7 design factors (at the top of the meta-model) can represent a performance loss or a potential performance gain. Working on design can help an organization, business unit or team increase its P2P Metric™ - for example increasing performance from 60% to 80% as in the diagram below. Ultimately working on design will enable a team and its members to spend more time in the Zone of Peak Performance™ (see Section 1).

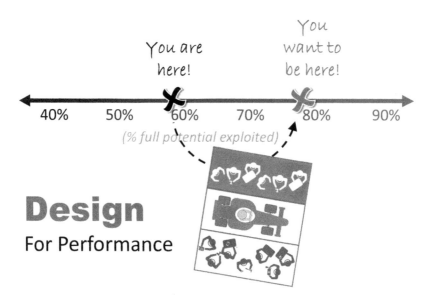

There is no such thing as **the perfect unit or team** – peak performing teams work at it continually. For example, a pit team will practice a pitstop about 70 times a week and the same again on the weekend of a race. Moreover, even great pit teams occasionally get it wrong. The issue of performance design and re-design is ongoing.

What is 'right' is very much situationally dependent, moreover it changes continuously over time. What is 'right' for one team may not be 'right' for another. The focus should be on what is **right for your team**, for your organisation and what it must achieve. What is 'right' **depends** on whether your team is a real team, what type of team it is, its size, and so on. It also depends on the stage that your team is at in its development. For example, whether your team is at the start, the middle or the end of its functional life.

The issue of design is not once-off, but rather ongoing. The requirements in terms of right people, in the right roles, doing the right work and so on, will change over time in response to the demands placed on the team from its stakeholders and its environment. **Organizations and teams must revisit their design on a regular basis**. Indeed, the best teams do this after every key project, workshop, or even meeting, using the questions about 'right people, right roles and so on' to reflect on performance and to identify opportunities for improvement.

Managers often see design as being a private matter - something for them to do alone. However, the highest performing teams are in fact **co-created where team members** are involved in discussions about design. The result is greater buy-in among team members, as well as insight from those closest to the action. Such design discussions are another approach to what is sometimes called team commissioning[90].

Design challenges don't fix themselves. Even if they settle down for a while, they will eventually come to the surface again. We struggle to find any organization or team from our research where a design problem righted itself without intervention. It seems to be a universal rule that if left unattended they get worse rather than better. For example, even if a 'problematic' team member leaves, the fundamental underlying issues that resulted in the problem not being proactively addressed will likely manifest in some other aspect of the team's management or design.

> *Every team is different, but the shared secret of teamwork is that it has to be worked at. Becoming a better team requires that you ask difficult questions, make tough choices and take action.*
> Khoi Tu[91]

SECTION 5:

COMPONENTS OF PERFORMANCE DESIGN

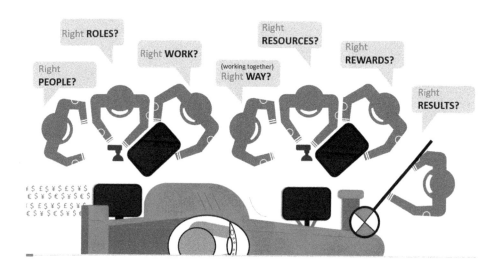

INTRODUCTION

In this section, we will explore the top of the meta-model and what it reveals about the importance of team set-up and design. That includes how factors such as Right People in the Right Roles can represent either a key source of performance losses, or gains.

Each design factor (e.g. Right People) is examined in overview, with details of where to go for more insights and tool at the end of this section.

FIRST THINGS FIRST

There is a double irony in the order of the seven dynamics:

- The first irony is that **Right Results should come first**, rather than last. Designing for performance should 'begin with the end in mind'[92] – that is the results to be achieved by the team. All other design factors pivot on the Right Results.

- The second irony is that **right people is number one, but shouldn't be**. This reflects the fact that most managers tend to overestimate the impact of the individual on performance and underestimate the impact of all other factors. This bias, called the Fundamental Misattribution Error, means we often rush to blame somebody without considering all the facts[93].

With the above in mind let's begin with the Right Results.

> We believe that the truly committed team is the most productive performance unit management has at its disposal—provided there are specific results for which the team is collectively responsible and provided the performance ethic of the company demands those results.
> Douglas Smith & Jon Katzenbach[94]

RIGHT RESULTS

In a pitstop it is the **result that matters most**. That means changing tires and making other adjustments, as quickly as possible, to get the car and driver back into the race with the maximum chances of winning.

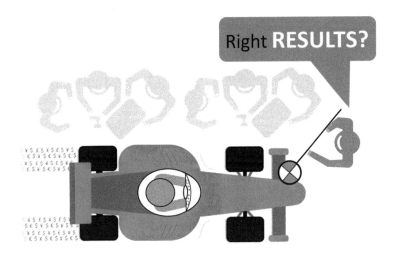

Measured in milliseconds, the results by which a pit team's performance is measured are clear to all. Moreover, they are clearly connected to winning. The same applies to all high-performing teams.

Q: How confident are you that your team is focusing on / delivering the RIGHT RESULTS?

Absolutely Not Confident	Not Confident	Average	Confident	Very Confident
☐	☐	☐	☐	☐

Right Results is arguably the most important of all the design factors. Yet, according to our benchmarking data, one in four teams (27%) are not sure that they are aiming for the Right Results, or that they can achieve them.

> *...you're just pushing to be the very best at what you do and use the newest technology and working with some of the brightest and best people in a team that's just so focused on one goal.*
> Bernadette Collins, Force India Team[95]

Look behind the labels at the top or the bottom of the Pitstop Meta-model™ and you will find up to a dozen related and interdependent variables. For example, in respect of 'Right People', the Pitstop Analytics™ solution explores issues such as diversity, number of high-performers, skills and talent development (see sample pages below).

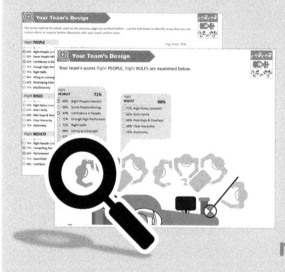

Looking behind the labels on the meta-model

RIGHT PEOPLE

Performance in the pit lane comes down to people. That is because despite the sophistication of F1™, pitstops are largely a manual affair. Yes, there are tools (jacks to lift the car and pneumatic wrenches to change the wheels), but success really depends on having the right people to get the job done.   The same applies to all teams. The question is:

Q: How confident are you that the RIGHT PEOPLE are on your team?

Absolutely Not Confident	Not Confident	Average	Confident	Very Confident
☐	☐	☐	☐	☐

Great teams are built with great people.   However, our benchmarking data puts the level of confidence in having the Right People at just 59%.   That is the equivalent of the driver pulling into the pit lane only to find that:

- Some of the pit team are missing
- Some of the pit team don't know or care much about the car, driver, or indeed winning the race.

Right people means right attitudes and skills. It can also mean the right personalities and styles too - not just for task effectiveness but also for the cohesiveness and social health of the team. If people are missing, or underperforming, a team will clearly struggle to reach its full performance potential.

> *For many good teams, superior talent is necessary; for great teams, though, it is insufficient. The central challenge of becoming a great team is to harness the full range of talent in the team; to make the whole greater than the sum of the parts and to know when 'we' beats 'I' and when 'I' matters more than 'we'.*
> Khoi Tu[96]

RIGHT ROLES

In the pit lane there are people to jack-up the car, to take the wheels off, to attach the new wheels, to replace the steering wheel (if required) and so on. Whether somebody's job is 'right rear wheel off' or 'front left wheel on' is very clear - it is reflected in where people stand around the car.

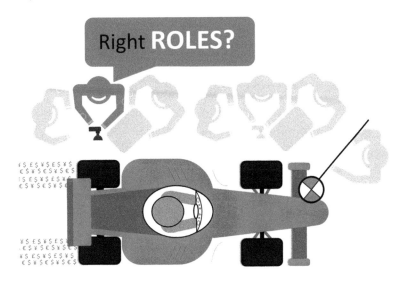

On a pit team, people are slotted into the role that best suits their level of experience and skill. There aren't two people vying to do the same role or any roles that are left unfilled. The question is:

Q: How confident are you that people are in the RIGHT ROLES on your team?

Absolutely Not Confident	Not Confident	Average	Confident	Very Confident
☐	☐	☐	☐	☐

On a pit team, all the roles are necessary for a successful pitstop – they are not just complimentary – they are interdependent. The car and driver cannot leave the pit lane until everybody's job has been done. So, imagine what happens within many organizations and teams, given Right Roles is rated at just 56% in our sample.

> *You try different roles – whatever role you excel at that is the role you will be given.*
> Joseph Haugh, *wheel gun man, Williams F1 Team pit crew*[97]

RIGHT WORK

For any team what matters most is the work that needs to be done. In the context of a pitstop that is clear to all involved - the job is to get the car and driver back into the race with the maximum chances of winning.

In the pitlane there is **little scope for ambiguity or confusion about what needs to be done.** Moreover, there is little margin for getting it wrong. The sequence of activities has been so precisely defined and regularly practiced as to enable the team to speedily complete them even in the most pressurized environment. If only other teams applied these principles.

Q: How confident are your team is doing the RIGHT WORK?

Absolutely Not Confident	Not Confident	Average	Confident	Very Confident
☐	☐	☐	☐	☐

For almost half of the teams (45%) in our analytics and research there are question marks regarding at least some aspect of the 'Right Work'. These teams are composed of busy and talented individuals – what a shame that their efforts are being misdirected. No matter how good a team is, it cannot truly perform, unless it is doing the right work.

> *The tasks that teams perform should be tasks that are best performed by a team.*
> Michael A. West[98]

RIGHT WAY (of Working Together)

Look at the top of the model - it is obvious that this team is working together in the right way. The right people are in the right roles and they are working together in an efficient manner. There are high levels of symmetry, co-ordination and interdependence. It just looks right!

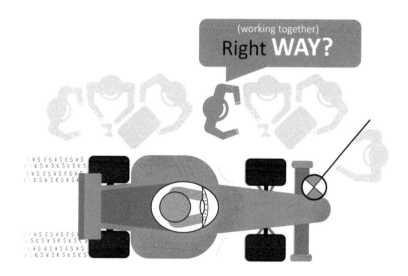

Most teams never realize their full potential because they don't work together in the Right Way. The question is:

Q: How confident are you that your team is working (together) in the RIGHT WAY?

Absolutely Not Confident	Not Confident	Average	Confident	Very Confident
☐	☐	☐	☐	☐

Most F1™ teams have the potential to pitstop in 2 seconds, or less. However, it doesn't always happen. If a pit team does not work together in the 'Right Way', the pitstop could take 5 seconds, 2 minutes or even 5 minutes! If it was to take 5 seconds that would be a performance loss of 3 seconds (5-2=3) and that is more than enough to lose a race. Yet, this is what is happening in 4 out of 10 teams in our sample because they don't work together in the 'Right Way'.

> *More organic than mechanical, members work together in ways that are collaborative, flexible, creative, and adaptive. They create just-enough-structure—at the time that it is needed—to support purpose and outcomes.*
> Geoffrey M. Bellman and Kathleen D. Ryan[99]

RIGHT RESOURCES

With mid-race refuelling presently banned, modern day pitstops focus on replacing the car's four wheels. So, an effective pitstop requires a supply of heated tires and the tools to put them on. Without them the team will fail.

Q: Are you confident that your team has the RIGHT RESOURCES?

Absolutely Not Confident	Not Confident	Average	Confident	Very Confident
☐	☐	☐	☐	☐

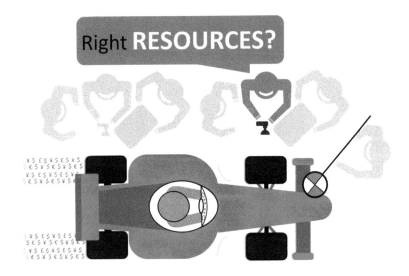

Most teams face resource constraints of one kind, or another. However, it is not just an abundance of resources that matters, but resourcefulness.

Our benchmarking data puts the level of confidence in respect of the Right Resources at 62%. That would be like sending a pit team to do its work without enough spare tires or the pneumatic wheel guns that are required to put them on.

> *...resource availability can greatly smooth a team's path... resource insufficiency can be disastrous, even for a team that is otherwise well directed, structured, and supported.*
> J. Richard Hackman[100]

RIGHT REWARDS

Behaviour is complex, so too is human motivation. It can be difficult to predict the behaviour of a single individual, not to talk about the behaviour of groups or crowds of people within organizations. In this context, trying to find the right rewards to shape behaviour is no easy matter.

You might be thinking any reward is better than none, but think again. Using the wrong reward can have a negative, rather than a positive, effect on performance.

Q: How confident are you that the RIGHT REWARDS are being used?

Absolutely Not Confident	Not Confident	Average	Confident	Very Confident
☐	☐	☐	☐	☐

Trying to find the right rewards to shape behaviour can be a challenge. As often as not organizations get it wrong. You might be thinking any reward is better than none, but think again. Using the wrong reward can have a negative, rather than a positive, effect on performance.

In Pitstop for Performance™ we use the latest performance analytics and behavioural analysis to explore the role of intrinsic and extrinsic rewards.

> *A fixed salary is not something that motivates performance. It motivates people to join and stay in the organization, but not to perform at a higher level.*
> Jay R. Galbraith[101]

There is a toolkit to help you unlock performance gains for each aspect of design (Right People, Right Roles and so on). Available online these incorporate the latest insights from social psychology, behavioural economics, organizational design and business leadership. Find out more at:

www.GrowthPitstop.com/shop

DESIGN Memory Test: Write as many of the labels as you can remember below. When you are finished check your answers against the inside front cover.

YOUR PERSONAL DESIGN?

Using the diagram overleaf, plot your own personal work design as per the example below.

Plot <u>yourself</u> on the **design** factors on the diagram below:

- There are 7 lines in the diagram – one for each design factor
- Each line has a Confidence scale from 0 to 10 (e.g. 10 = 'Very Confident')
- Put an '**X**' on each line, join them and shade to the circumference to highlight the potential (see example)

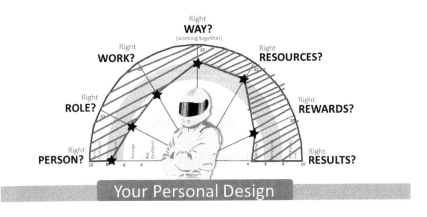

Right
WAY?
(working together)

Right
WORK?

Right
RESOURCES?

Right
ROLE?

Right
REWARDS?

Right
PERSON?

Right
RESULTS?

Your Personal Design

Complete the diagram and discuss it with a trusted colleague or coach. What does your completed diagram (overleaf) reveal about your personal work set-up or design at this time? Does it reveal any performance losses or potential for gain?

Plot yourself on the design factors on the diagram below:

- There are 7 lines in the diagram – one for each design factor
- Each line has a Confidence scale from 0 to 10 (e.g. 10 = 'Very Confident')
- Put an 'X' on each line, join them and shade to the circumference to highlight the potential (see example)

Right **WAY?**
(working with colleagues)

Right **RESOURCES?**

Right **REWARDS?**

Right **RESULTS?**

Right **WORK?**

Right **ROLE?**

Right **PERSON?**

Very Confident

Confident

Average

Not Confident

Very Un-confident

Your Personal Design

WHAT WILL YOU DO NEXT?

Having reviewed the 7 design variables at a high level, take a moment to reflect on the implications. Specifically, which ones, if worked upon, would have the greatest impact on your performance and well-being, as well as that of your team. To help you the model showing all the design variables is presented again overleaf.

When you have selected a particular Design factor can access tools and insights to help online at: www.GrowthPitstop.com/shop.

Not sure if you need to work on design? Use the Pitstop Analytics™ to assess and benchmark your organization/team's design. See: www.GrowthPitstop.com/analytics

Performance Design: What aspects of your team's design will you focus on?

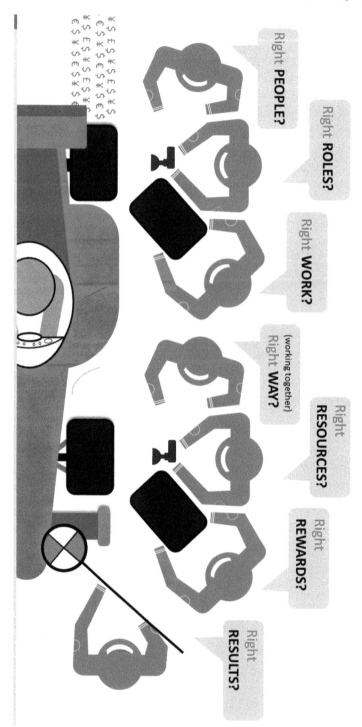

Part 2:

POOR PERFORMING TEAM

Exploring the bottom of the model, including:

- The causes of team underperformance and dysfunction
- The attitudes and behaviours (i.e. dynamics) of effective teams
- Key dynamics (urgency, communication, trust, etc.)

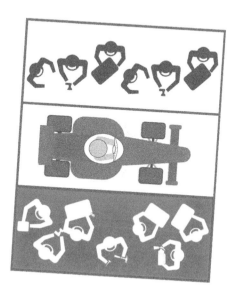

SECTION 6:

THE DYNAMICS OF POOR PERFORMANCE

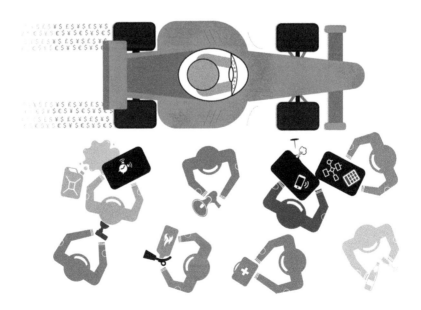

INTRODUCTION

In this section we will tell the story of the underperforming pit team – the one that causes the driver and team to lose the race. It is lap 22 and the driver has a 900-meter lead, but a change of tires can no longer be put off. It is time to pitstop. The driver pulls into the pitlane and stops on the mark. For the next few seconds success is in the hands of the pit team.

Conscious that every millisecond counts the driver looks aghast as the pit team descends into chaos. At the back-right wheel, team member 1 recklessly knocks over a can of oil in the rush to get the wheel on (see below). Worried that the white-hot heat of the car's disk brakes or engine could ignite the spill, team member 3 rushes over with the fire-extinguisher.

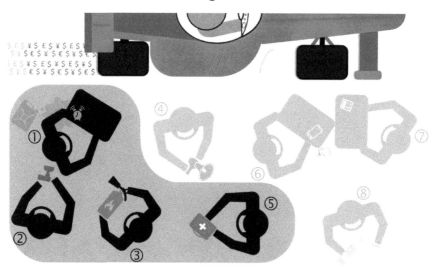

The car cannot leave until all four tires have been replaced, but it is hard to see how that is going to happen. There is only one pneumatic wheel wrench and it is in the hands of 'a nutter' (2) who is about to apply it to the back of another team member's (1) head. Spotting the danger, team member 5 rushes to the rescue with the first-aid kit. The driver looks on in disbelief, blood pressure rising. At the front of the car there is more chaos (shown in the next diagram). In an attempt to regain control, team member 4 has taken to shouting instructions over a loudhailer. But nobody is listening. Team members 6 and 7 are busy jostling to put on a new wheel, not realizing that the old wheel is still attached to the car. Moreover, team member 6 is oblivious to a puncture in the wheel, probably the result of sabotage!

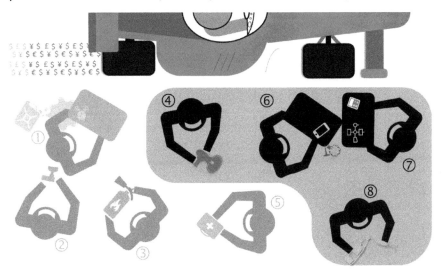

As the milliseconds turn into seconds and then into minutes, competitor cars race by. Meanwhile team members are busy competing with each other. There is conflict rather than cooperation, resulting in duplication, inefficiency and waste. There is even danger. This is a team that cannot win. Team member 8 has given up on the team and is selfishly drinking the Champagne. Clearly, this team is a mess! Now let's do a more technical or scientific analysis of this team's performance, drawing out the implications for teams within organizations.

TECHNICALLY SPEAKING

When it comes to performance the picture at the bottom of the meta-model paints a thousand words. Those words, contrast the difference between a peak performing team and a clumsy group, or the top and bottom of the meta-model, as shown in the table below.

	TOP of the Meta-Model	BOTTOM Meta-Model
What is it?	Peak Performing Team	Dysfunctional Group or Crowd of Individuals.
Purpose	Everybody is working towards a common purpose – to win.	No common purpose. Everybody is pulling in different directions.
Teamwork	Coordination and cooperation. High levels of interdependence.	Conflict and competition. Everybody is doing their own thing.
Output	Team output is significantly greater than sum of individuals.	Poor output. People would achieve more working alone.
Design (see Section 4)	Right people are in the right roles, doing the right work, etc.	There is confusion about roles, results, way of working, etc.

Technically speaking the group at the bottom of the meta-model is **'co-acting' in the same space, but exhibits independence,**

rather than interdependence[102]. In the absence of a common purpose, everybody is doing their own thing. There is competition rather than collaboration, with poor co-ordination and communication. That is why we say that the bottom of the meta-model is a group, rather than a team (or at least a real team).

The stark difference between the top and the bottom of the model is a visual way of communicating the difference between a group (bottom of meta-model or right column of the table) and a team / peak performing team (top of meta-model or left column). The bottom of the meta-model is in direct contrast to the order, structure and synchronised teamwork we saw at the top of the meta-model where the right people are in the right roles working together in the right way and so on.

There are advantages and disadvantages to all collaborative activity, but at the bottom of model the disadvantages clearly outweigh the advantages. As noted earlier, the more technical term for these are process losses, or simply performance losses. The number one source of these losses is the inability, or the unwillingness, of people to work together. **Performance losses are rife in this group** - to such an extent that people could probably achieve more by acting alone.

The chaotic interaction among team members at the bottom of the meta-model is clear evidence of poor social health within this team, but with **real implications for task performance**. All this messiness inevitably gets in the way of doing the work, with only 3 of the 8 team members doing the work of a pit team (or at least trying to do it). In this way, the team's task performance and social health are clearly intertwined – as shown overleaf.

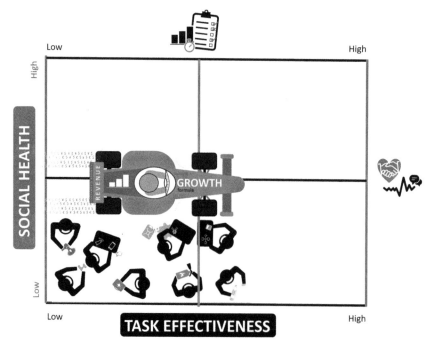

If the social health of a team is poor, its task related performance must suffer. The messy stuff - personalities, politics and so on – will inevitably detract from getting the work done.

Primary or Secondary?

Some researchers and writers on the topic of teams suggest that the dynamics of a team – the behavioral interplay between team members – is secondary to performance. They argue that getting the design right is the manager's top priority. Clearly, poor design has an important role to play in the chaos at the bottom of the model. However, the dysfunctional dynamics among team members exacerbates the problem and has itself a dramatic impact on performance. When it comes to team performance we argue that **design and dynamics have equal billing – they both matter and must be worked on in tandem.**

IT'S A MESS!

Let's switch out of the technical mode. In everyday language, the bottom of the meta-model is a mess. People are 'all over the place' with clear evidence of waste, conflict and even danger. But what would you do with such a team? Would you try to fix it, disband it or resign to accepting it?

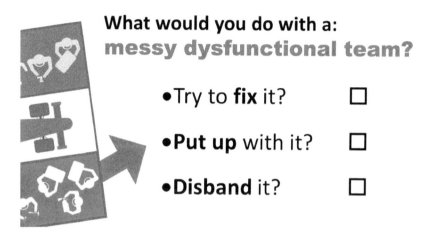

What would you do with a:
messy dysfunctional team?

- Try to **fix** it? ☐

- **Put up** with it? ☐

- **Disband** it? ☐

Most managers might be tempted to throw their arms up in the air and **simply give up on such a team**. This would be exhibited in behavior such as bringing the team together less often, reverting to a command and control style of management, failing to address behavioral dysfunction within the team, sweeping tensions under the rug and so on. But when managers show (by their behavior) that they don't trust, or value a team they send a signal to others (including team members). The result is often a spiral of disinterest or disillusionment and a further deterioration of team dynamics and ultimately performance.

Managers have traditionally spent their time focused on what is typically called the 'hard stuff' – that is the strategies, processes, systems and so on, but neglect dynamics (the so called 'soft stuff'[103]). Working on strategies, spreadsheets and systems is easier than engaging in what can be an uncomfortable and risky area, one for which most managers have not been trained. Too often we see issues of team dynamics left to fester. But avoidance is rarely the best strategy, not least because, **left unattended, team dynamics typically gets worse rather than better**. Moreover, poor dynamics can be contagious – spilling over to other areas of the organization.

> *Poor collaboration is a disease afflicting even the best companies.*
> Morten Hansen[104]

EMBRACE THE MESS!

Most managers who see a dysfunctional team in the pit lane want to take off faster than a fast car. That would be a mistake because there is money in the mess! The performance losses that result from poor team dynamics are burning your organization's money.

In times gone by, the dynamics within an organization or team might have been labelled 'culture' or 'soft stuff' and dismissed as 'touchy-feely'. In more recent times they have been called 'organizational health' and linked to the bottom line[105]. Indeed, data from leading institutions, such as Harvard[106], and consulting houses, such as McKinsey[107], suggests that culture, or 'organizational health' accounts for as much as 50% of performance. It may therefore be more important than talent, knowledge, or innovation[108].

As the CEO of one of our network partners says; 'this stuff may no longer be soft and fluffy, but it will always be messy'. What he means is that teams and teamwork is **no longer an organizational nice to have – a cultural aspiration, or style of leadership**. It is not just about creating a great place to work, treating all employees with dignity and respect, or other philanthropic values. Rather, it is a hard-nosed and pragmatic business decision – an essential strategy for growth, performance and innovation which recognizes that organizational and team performance are inextricably intertwined.

Bottom of the meta-model:

Embrace
The MESS!

If this section had a subtitle it would be; 'embrace the mess.' Such a mess as that shown at the bottom of the meta-model is likely to represent a significant financial cost to the organization, as well as a personal cost to the people involved. So much so that it cannot be avoided - dealing with the mess is a priority. Not to attempt to fix a messed-up and underperforming team (or at least disband it) is a serious miscalculation. Not only is it a drain on organizational performance and a drag on individual team members, but it sends the wrong signal organization-wide regarding culture and performance. The advice for managers is to get comfortable with the mess - indeed to embrace it. Failing to manage poor dynamics poses an existential threat to the viability of teams, as well as the long-term survival of organizations. The message for managers is: if you neglect dynamics, you neglect your organization.

> *...Sometimes group dynamics get complicated and messy—but that's OK.*
> Geoffrey M. Bellman and Kathleen D. Ryan[6]

IT AIN'T NATURAL

A peak performing team, such as that shown at the top of the meta-model, is a source of pride and inspiration. By contrast a messy team, such as that at the bottom of the meta-model, is a cause of frustration and disappointment. Moreover, it is something that many managers feel helplessness to do anything about. But why get frustrated by something that is entirely natural?

> *The fact remains that teams, because they are made up of imperfect human beings, are inherently dysfunctional.*
> Patrick Lencioni[109]

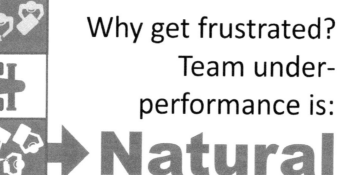

Why get frustrated? Team under-performance is:

Natural

The group or crowd at the bottom of the meta-model is messy, but it is real. Indeed, compared to the top of the model, it is probably a more accurate description of the reality of teamwork in most organizations. It is a recurring theme of this book that high performing teams are far from the norm. Indeed, you could say that, in the context of most organizations, they are unnatural.

It is worth repeating: **Effective teamwork isn't natural**. Yes, anthropologists say that the ability to work in teams has been key to the survival and ultimately the success of our species. However, the same evolutionary process that has enabled human cooperation and trust is as likely to result in competition and suspicion[110]. This is particularly the case if people are not like us[111]. Moreover, effective teamwork is counter-cultural in most of our organizations, as well as our broader societies.

All this leads us back to the question:

Q: Why get frustrated by something – the challenges of teams
- that is simply natural?

A team will underperform unless you, or somebody else, is prepared to do something about it. A peak performing team is no accident – it must be carefully designed for effective task performance and the dynamics of healthy team interactions carefully nurtured. The good news is that although teaming is not natural, working effectively in teams is an ability that can be fostered by organizations and learned by all[112].

Bottom of the meta-model:

Ability **to work in/with teams so as to drive success**

Team-ability

The bottom of the meta-model defines team-ability by highlighting eight behaviors and attitudes that are required for effective teamwork and collaboration. We call them behavioral dynamics.

> *...people have to learn to team; it doesn't come naturally in most organizations. Teaming is worth learning, because it is essential for improvement, problem solving, and innovation in a functioning enterprise.*
> Amy C. Edmondson[113]

BEHAVIORAL DYNAMICS

Our extensive research identifies 8 key attitudes and behaviors that determine the ability to team. We call them behavioural dynamics, or dynamics for short. These are the cognitive and behavioural patterns that govern how team members work and interact.

Bottom of the meta-model:

The psychology & behavior that drives the performance of individuals & teams

Dynamics

The use of the term 'dynamics' is inspired by the fields of Group Dynamics[114] and Systems Dynamics[115]. These are essential to understanding performance at an individual, team and organizational level. Each member of the pit team at the bottom of the meta-model represents one of the 8 dynamics and is labelled accordingly (as shown overleaf). Use the diagram to identify those behaviors that represent strengths for your team, as well as any opportunities for improvement.

> *Creating high performance teams requires that we pay heed not only to the structures and processes that facilitate team working but also to the more messy aspects of teamwork.*
> Manfred F. R. Kets de Vries[116]

Organizational & Team Dynamics: Rank them in order of importance to your team.

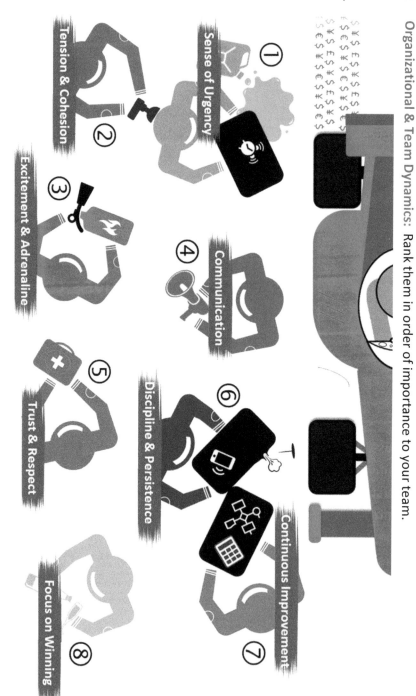

1. Sense of Urgency
2. Tension & Cohesion
3. Excitement & Adrenaline
4. Communication
5. Trust & Respect
6. Discipline & Persistence
7. Continuous Improvement
8. Focus on Winning

When it comes to teamwork a picture paints a thousand words, so take a moment to study the model on the previous page. From the visual you can see the following counterproductive, even destructive, behaviors (with the corresponding team member number in brackets):

Conflict (1 & 2)	Shouting (4)
Competition (7 & 8)	Waste (1 & 8)
Distractions (1, 2, 6 & 7)	Rescuing (3 & 5)
Duplication (7 & 8)	Recklessness (1 & 2)
Selfishness (6)	Solo-runs (1, 2, 7 & 8)
Firefighting (3)	Disengagement (6)

Q: How many of these behaviors can you spot in your team or group?

The above dysfunctions represent process losses. They are just some of the reasons why it is often said that 'bad collaboration is worse than no collaboration at all'[117]. The group or team at the bottom of the meta-model spends too much time on its internal dynamics and not enough on the requirements of its external environment, its stakeholders and ultimately its purpose. This so-called team isn't winning, neither are the people on it. Chances are they would rather be somewhere else. Confronted by such a team, the driver will be reluctant to pull the car in to the pit lane, hoping that the tires and everything else will hold out.

Research consistently shows that teams under-perform…
…having a team is often worse than having no team at all.
Richard Hackman[118]

TEST YOUR TEAM DYNAMICS

Has your organization / team got the dynamics required for performance and success?   Find out by rating your organization/team's dynamics using the following table.

Dynamic	Very Poor = 1, Very Good = 5 (circle as appropriate below)				
Sense of Urgency	1	2	3	4	5
Tension and Cohesion	1	2	3	4	5
Excitement & Adrenaline	1	2	3	4	5
Communication	1	2	3	4	5
Trust & Respect	1	2	3	4	5
Discipline & Persistence	1	2	3	4	5
Continuous Improvement	1	2	3	4	5
Focus on Winning	1	2	3	4	5

The above is essentially an audit of culture or organizational health. Teams must exhibit these 8 dynamics. The organizational environment must foster them also. With this in mind, let's add up your organization/team's score for dynamics:

Score	What it means:
35-40:	The behaviors and attitudes within your team are consistent with a peak performing team.
25-34:	While your team's dynamics are overall good, there are some opportunities for improvement. These should translate into gains in task effectiveness and social health.
15-24:	Your team's dynamics are not consistent with the behaviors required for effective teamwork. They are indicative of a group, rather than a team. The

	result is likely to be significant performance losses.
<15:	These are the dynamics of dysfunction and suggest that the costs of teamwork may exceed the benefits. It is time to go back to the drawing board and to revisit the design of the team.

Look in the Mirror

When managers look at the list of dynamics they can quickly identify the gaps or shortcomings among their teams. What they often overlook however is their own. For example, one CEO immediately highlighted Urgency and Discipline as deficiencies among his team. As he did, people were thinking 'what about your own discipline and persistence?' The CEO was known to flit from priority to priority - launching enthusiastically into the next 'big thing', while dropping last week or last month's 'big thing' in the process. People looked at each other with a 'here we go again' expression, but nobody said anything. To the CEO, their silence was further evidence that his team just didn't get it. A psychologist would probably say that this is a classic case of transference - where the leader projected his own personal insecurities onto the team. Regardless of what you call it, we see it happening all the time. The most important dynamic is often the one that gets overlooked - that is the leader's own behavior and attitudes. You will have an opportunity to score your own dynamics at the end of the next section.

A DYNAMIC APPROACH TO CULTURE

Team dynamics is a re-framing of the concept of organizational or team culture. It is a new approach to a topic that has traditionally left managers feeling helpless and frustrated. Most managers believe that culture is critical to business success perhaps even more important than strategy, or operating model[119]. They agree with the popular saying that; 'culture eats strategy for breakfast'.[120] Yet, ask managers to define culture, much less to spell out how it should be managed, and the result is confusion[121]. Most managers say that their organization's culture needs to change[122], but where to start? Culture is a somewhat nebulous concept – one that is difficult to link to specific behaviors within an organization, or team[123]. Thus, it has traditionally been difficult to measure or even manage.

> ...there is little consensus on what organizational culture actually is, never mind how it influences behavior and whether it is something leaders can change.
> Michael D. Watkins[124]

The good news is that culture is undergoing a make-over. By re-labelling it as 'behavioural dynamics' and focusing on a 'few critical behaviors'[125] culture now comes under the control of managers and their teams.

> Achieving strategic goals and accelerating performance results often requires that employees at multiple levels of the organization change certain critical behaviors.
> Jon Katzenbach, Laird Post, et al.[126]

Focusing on
Critical Behaviors

The eight behavioural dynamics are a tangible manifestation of an organization or team's culture – its 'behavioural signature'[127] as it were. That is its norms of behaviour and system of beliefs - its way of doing things and of relating to the world. They are **specific attitudes and behaviors that can be observed, measured and indeed shaped**. This is one of the reasons for re-labelling culture as 'dynamics' - to recognise that it is dynamic – that it is evolving, and that it can change. It is a dynamic approach to culture which zooms in on the critical attitudes and behaviors that, if changed, would have a major impact on the performance of the organization or team, as well as the interactions of its individuals and teams.

The workplace is a complex social system[128] with terms such as 'relationship soup'[129] and 'emotional stew'[130] being used to describe the complexity of workplace interactions. The focus on specific behaviours and attitudes from the list of 8 dynamics is an essential primer for action. In selecting a particular dynamic(s) to work upon, you might consider the impact that it could have on the performance and well-being of your team:

*Q.1: What **critical dynamic(s)** (from the 8 listed/modelled earlier) does your organization or team most need to work on?*

If your organization is having trouble teaming then watch out. Teams are the canary in the mine of organizational health. If they are not working then it is likely an indicator of more fundamental problems; cultural, strategic or structural.

Teaming is...

The 'Canary in the mine' of Organizational Health

The same environmental factors that inhibit effective teamwork, will also hinder individual and organizational performance. If people can't share information, engage with alternative perspectives or co-operate with others when they are supposed to be working in teams, they probably won't do it at other times either. As examined in our other book 'Teams Don't Work', an environment that encourages individualism, internal competition and solo-runs is not just bad for teams, it is bad for business.

How Dynamics Shape Performance

Traditionally team design was most closely associated with task effectiveness and behavior associated with social health. The table below shows the widespread effect of the key behavioral dynamics on the 4 dimensions of team performance: Task, Decision, Social and Development. This relates to the view of performance 'in the round' examined in the 'lollipop model'[131]. The dark circles indicate where the impact has a direct impact on performance, while the hollow circle indicates where the impact is indirect.

	Task Effectiveness	Decision Accuracy	Social Health	Development Potential
Sense of Urgency	●	●	○	○
Tension & Cohesion	●	●	●	●
Excitement & Adrenaline	●	●	●	○
Communication	●	●	●	○
Trust & Respect	○	●	●	○
Discipline & Persistence	●	○	○	●
Continuous Improvement	●	●	●	●
Everybody Wins	○	○	●	○

Don't let culture eat strategy for breakfast. Have them feed each other.
Ken Favaro[132]

MANAGING DYNAMICS

To identify behaviors that should be changed is easy, but to successfully change them is not. Mandating a change in behaviour or attitude is rarely enough[133]. That is because much of the dynamics within teams happen beneath the iceberg of conscious awareness. They are often the result, not of conscious decision, but of routine and habit. Because they are both hidden and yet deeply ingrained, changing behaviors is not easy. For a start, managers must go beneath the surface to understand organizational or team dynamics. They must engage with emotions as well as with logic and fact. Moreover, because the dynamics of an organization or team reveals a lot about its manager, he or she must look within, as well as without.

 Team Dynamics: The Tip of the Iceberg

Go beneath the surface!

Contrary to conventional wisdom the culture or dynamics of an organization can be measured and managed. Indeed, measurement and management of the eight key dynamics is essential.   Although it is typical to say that change isn't easy, casting the light of awareness on attitudes and behaviors within a team is an important first step towards change.   To help in the process there are, for example, many tools to measure culture or organizational health, including our own performance analytics product (see Appendix).   But even simple steps help.   For example, asking a few awareness-building questions (at the end of each team meeting) can be powerful:

- How did we meet today as a team?
- What behaviors will we keep for the next meeting?
- What behaviors will we leave behind?
- What emotions were present?
- Which emotions/behaviors were helpful/unhelpful?

> *The mere act of repeatedly measuring performance and concomitant behavior shifts can act as a powerful driver of change and a reminder of target behaviors.*
> Jon Katzenbach, Laird Post, et al[134]

DYNAMICS BY DESIGN

It is important to remember that the **design and dynamics perspectives on team performance are complementary**, rather than competing.

So, if you are spending a lot of time dealing with petty squabbles, or dealing with personality and politics within your team, look at the design of your team. If the wrong people are in the wrong roles and doing the wrong work, the dynamics of the organization or team must inevitably suffer.

Many of the problems in terms of dynamics are a response to poor team, task and even organizational design. Making changes to design can interrupt patterns of disruptive behavior, while tackling the underlying structural problems that put people at odds with each other. These include ambiguous or conflicting roles, ways of working, as well as means of measuring results. With this in mind, take a moment to look back at the table where you scored the design factors for your team (Section 4).

Q: What design variables impact negatively on the behavioral dynamics of your team?

What does the way you rate your team's dynamics say about you? Well perhaps a lot. For example, Type A[135] personalities - those whose personalities are more competitive, outgoing, ambitious, impatient and/or aggressive - will often focus on urgency, excitement and adrenaline as gaps, while more relaxed Type B personalities may be more likely to focus on trust and respect, everybody is winning and communication.

WHERE TO NEXT?

Any of the 8 dynamics (at the bottom of the meta-model) can represent a performance loss or a potential performance gain. Working on dynamics can help an organization, business unit or team increase its P2P Metric™ - for example from 60% to 80% as in the diagram below. Ultimately working on design will enable a team and its members to spend more time in the Zone of Peak Performance™ (see Section 1).

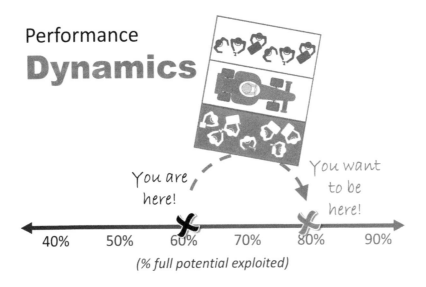

Pick a dynamic that is importance to your team at this time and set goals for its improvement. However, do keep in mind that all of the dynamics, just like the members of a peak performing team, are interdependent and connected. For example:

- Poor Communication is typically accompanied by issues of Trust & Respect, as well as Tension & Cohesion.

- Discipline & Persistence is often linked with a Sense of Urgency, as well as Excitement & Adrenaline.

- Continuous Improvement, tends to be fostered by Trust & Respect and fueled by Excitement & Adrenaline.

As the above examples suggest, problems with respect to dynamics come in twos and threes. The implication is that you cannot just work on improving any one behavioural dynamic on its own.

SECTION 7:

COMPONENTS OF
PERFORMANCE DYNAMICS

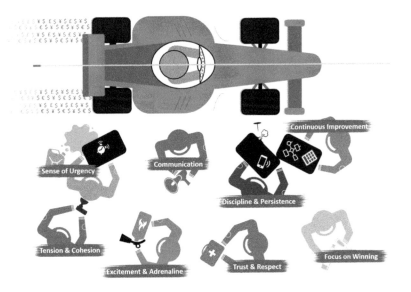

INTRODUCTION

In this section we will present a summary overview of the 8 Dynamics at the bottom of the meta model. The objective is to identify those behavioural dynamics that represent a performance loss or potential performance gains for your organisation or team.

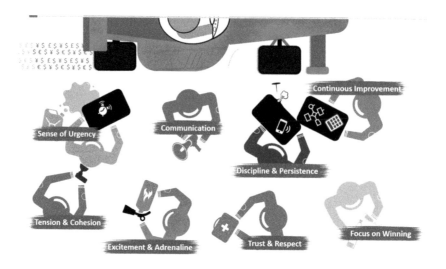

In this section, you will find a one-page overview of each of the 8 dynamics. Each dynamic (e.g. Communication) is examined in overview. Then in Section 8: Focus on Winning you will find a sample of the additional tools and information available for each of the dynamics. For more visit: www.GrowthPitstop.com/shop

SENSE OF URGENCY

There is a real sense of urgency in the pit lane. There is not a millisecond to lose in getting the car and driver back into the race. Yet, pit team members exhibit a certain calmness. Like all high performing teams, they must balance the need for speed with the need for effective execution.

Sense of Urgency

Q: How would you rate your team's level of urgency?

Very Poor	Poor	Average	Good	Very Good
☐	☐	☐	☐	☐

What is the single biggest error people make when they try to change? After reflection, I decided the answer was that they did not create a high enough sense of urgency.
J.P. Kotter[136]

Some organizations and teams are ruled by a stop watch, others are run by an hourglass. Getting the balance right between the two is key to achieving and sustaining high levels of performance.

Look behind the labels at the bottom of the Pitstop Meta-model™ and you will find up to a dozen related and interdependent variables. These are explored in Pitstop Programs and via the Pitstop Analytics™ (as shown in the sample page below).

Looking behind the labels on the meta-model

EXCITEMENT & ADRENALINE

Midrace the pit team waits primed and ready for action. Then the call is given 'box, box, box' - the driver will enter the pit lane on the next lap.

Adrenaline & Excitement

As the car approaches the team springs into action. Adrenaline is pumping - fingers are twitching and hearts are beating.   For a few seconds all eyes will be on the team - staying calm is essential! The question is:

Q: How would you rate your team's level of excitement & adrenaline?

Very Poor	Poor	Average	Good	Very Good
☐	☐	☐	☐	☐

Much has been written about the importance of mission, vision and purpose. But for many, these words have lost their meaning. Today, it is more fashionable to talk about passion, energy and engagement. That is what Adrenaline & Excitement is all about. But take care – sustaining the right level of adrenaline can be a challenge and too much can be dangerous.

> *What are today's scarce resources, the new sources of competitive advantage? For most companies, the truly scarce resources are the time, talent, and energy of their people, and the ideas those people generate and implement.*
> Michael C. Mankins & Eric Garton[137]

TENSION & COHESION

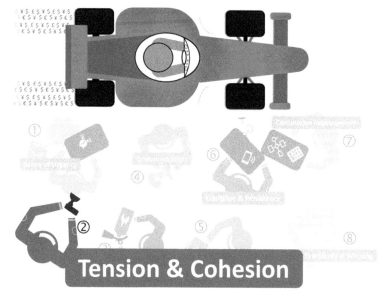

The pit team is a cohesive unit of performance, working effectively together to achieve a common goal in a tense environment where the work is complex and the pressure on time is intense. It is this balance of tension and cohesion that makes the pit team such a powerful metaphor for team performance.

At this moment, there are two opposing forces acting on your team. One is pulling your team members more tightly together. The other is threatening to push them apart. These countervailing forces are Tension and Cohesion. The question is:

Q: How would you rate your team's level of tension and cohesion?

Very Poor	Poor	Average	Good	Very Good
☐	☐	☐	☐	☐

When it comes to collaboration, sometimes managers hope things will go well but do not fully appreciate the costs of working across the organization and resolving conflict.
Morten Hansen[138]

COMMUNICATION

Communication is easy in relaxed environments where people are not under the pressure of deadlines or targets. However, turn up the pressure and communication becomes more difficult. The pit lane is a perfect metaphor for the challenges of maintaining effective communication in high pressure noisy environments.

Q: How would you rate the effectiveness of your team's communication?

Very Poor	Poor	Average	Good	Very Good
☐	☐	☐	☐	☐

Teams don't have problems having the nice conversations, but for many there are important conversations that are being avoided. Indeed, if there is a red or amber in terms of the design or the dynamics of a team (i.e. top or bottom of the pitstop meta-model) there is likely a conversation that needs to happen.

> *...we've found patterns of communication to be the most important predictor of a team's success. Not only that, but they are as significant as all the other factors - individual intelligence, personality, skill, and the substance of discussions — combined.*
> Alex "Sandy" Pentland[139]

TRUST & RESPECT

Racing is obviously a dangerous sport and the pit lane can be a dangerous place to work, with fast moving cars, heavy lifting and of course lots of noise. Paradoxically, F1™ is leading the way in terms of Health and Safety[140].

Safety is just as important to organizations and teams, because high performance requires the creation of an environment of safety, trust and respect. The question is:

Q: How would you rate the level of trust and respect within your team and its environment?

Very Poor	Poor	Average	Good	Very Good
☐	☐	☐	☐	☐

Trust & Respect

The term psychological safety describes a climate in which people feel free to express relevant thoughts and feelings without fear of being penalized.
Amy C. Edmondson[141]

DISCIPLINE & PERSISTENCE

Pit team members are disciplined athletes. In the run-up to each race they will practice as many as one hundred pit stops. Team members will also spend countless hours training in the gym. They have stamina, grit and determination.

Discipline & Persistence

Peak performing teams are not merely gifted for greatness. Yes, they may have an abundance of talent and skill, but that alone is not enough. To have a fighting chance of winning there are two other important characteristics required. They are discipline and persistence. The question is:

Q: How would you rate your team's level of discipline & persistence?

Very Poor	Poor	Average	Good	Very Good
☐	☐	☐	☐	☐

A collection of talented individuals without personal discipline will ultimately and inevitably fail.
James Kerr[142]

CONTINUOUS IMPROVEMENT

Far from the Winner's Podium, the Champagne and the Press Interviews, is the real secret of success in F1™. It is a commitment to continuous improvement that involves the relentless pursuit of

the millisecond advantage. It defines an approach to performance management, learning and innovation that is dramatically different to that found in most organizations.

Q: How would you rate your team's commitment to Continuous Improvement?

Very Poor	Poor	Average	Good	Very Good
☐	☐	☐	☐	☐

> ...*most people are spending time and energy covering up their weaknesses, managing other people's impressions of them, showing themselves to their best advantage, playing politics, hiding their inadequacies, hiding their uncertainties, hiding their limitations. Hiding.*
> Robert Kegan & Lisa Laskow Lahey[143]

FOCUS ON WINNING

F1™ is all about winning. So too is business. Yet managers often struggle to arrive at a definition of winning that resonates throughout their organization or even across their management team.   Moreover, they don't obsess about, recognize and celebrate winning to the same extent as race teams and their fans do.

Like most other cars, F1™ racing machines run on petrol. But that is only half the story. There is an even more combustible fuel that powers winning F1™ drivers and teams – the desire to win!   The same applies in all team and individual endeavours. The question is:

Q: How would you rate your team's focus on winning?

Very Poor	Poor	Average	Good	Very Good
☐	☐	☐	☐	☐

The next section will showcase the 'winning' dynamic in more detail.

> *For a team to make this transition, every member must look deeply at him- or herself to answer the basic question: What does it mean to be a player in this organization and on this team? If the answer is anything short of "It's about us winning," then the team is not even close to becoming great.*
> Howard M. Guttman[144]

DYNAMICS Memory Test: Write as many of the labels as you can remember below. When you are finished check your answers against the inside back cover.

YOUR PERSONAL DYNAMICS?

Using the diagram overleaf, plot your own personal work dynamics as per the example below.

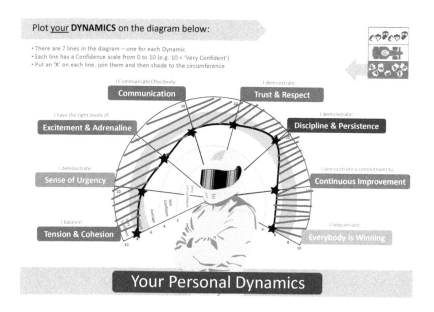

Complete the diagram and discuss it with a trusted colleague or coach. What does your completed diagram (overleaf) reveal about your personal work-related dynamics at this time? Does it reveal any performance losses, or potential performance gains?

Plot your DYNAMICS on the diagram below:

- There are 8 lines in the diagram – one for each Dynamic
- Each line has a Confidence scale from 0 to 10 (e.g. 10 = 'Very Confident')
- Put an 'X' on each line, join them and then shade to the circumference (see example)

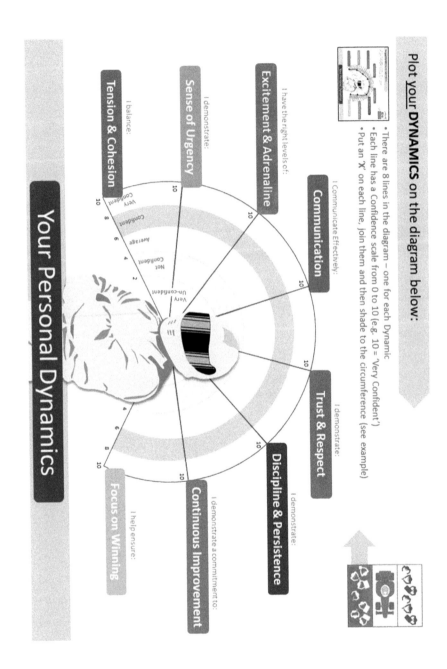

Your Personal Dynamics

Excitement & Adrenaline
I have the right levels of:

Sense of Urgency
I demonstrate:

Tension & Cohesion
I balance:

Communication
I Communicate Effectively:

Trust & Respect
I demonstrate:

Discipline & Persistence
I demonstrate:

Continuous Improvement
I demonstrate a commitment to:

Focus on Winning
I help ensure:

Very Confident
Confident
Average
Not Confident
Very Un-confident

10 8 6 4 2 4 6 8 10

WHAT WILL YOU DO NEXT?

Having reviewed the 8 dynamics at a high level, take a moment to reflect on the implications. Specifically, what behavior(s), if worked upon, would have the greatest impact on your performance and well-being, as well as that of your team. To help you the model showing all the behavioural dynamics is presented again overleaf.

When you have selected a particular Dynamic to work on, access tools and insights on it by visiting www.GrowthPitstop.com/shop.

Not sure if you need to work on dynamics?
Use the Pitstop Analytics™ to assess and benchmark your organization/team's dynamics. See:
www.GrowthPitstop.com/analytics

Organizational & Team Dynamics: Which behaviour(s) will you focus on? Circle them below:

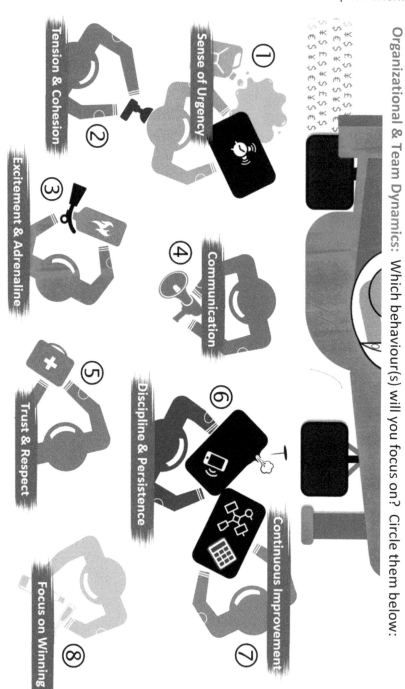

1. Sense of Urgency
2. Tension & Cohesion
3. Excitement & Adrenaline
4. Communication
5. Trust & Respect
6. Discipline & Persistence
7. Continuous Improvement
8. Focus on Winning

SAMPLE SECTION 8:

FOCUS ON WINNING

This Section takes one of the Dynamics – 'Focus on Winning' – and presents a sample of the insights and tool available for each of the 7 Design factors and 8 Dynamics at the top and bottom of the pitstop meta-model. For more information visit: www.GrowthPitstop.com/shop

INTRODUCTION

F1™ is all about winning. So too is business. Yet managers often struggle to arrive at a definition of winning that resonates throughout their organization or even across their management team. Moreover, they don't obsess about, recognize and celebrate winning to the same extent as race teams and their fans do. The question is:

Q: How would you rate your team's focus on winning?

Very Poor	Poor	Average	Good	Very Good
☐	☐	☐	☐	☐

Like most other cars, F1™ racing machines run on petrol. But that is only half the story. There is an even more combustible fuel that powers winning F1™ drivers and teams – the desire to win!   The same applies in all team and individual endeavours. Yet managers often struggle to arrive at a definition of winning that resonates throughout their organization or even across their management team. Moreover, they don't obsess about, recognize and celebrate winning to the same extent as race teams and their fans do. Putting winning back at the center of your projects, teams and strategies has the potential to unlock a new level of excitement, passion and performance.

> *For a team to make this transition, every member must look deeply at him- or herself to answer the basic question: What does it mean to be a player in this organization and on this team? If the answer is anything short of "It's about us winning," then the team is not even close to becoming great.*
> Howard M. Guttman[145]

WINNING PARALLELS FOR MANAGERS

An obsession with winning characterizes F1™. Winning requires great ambition combined with intense focus. There are several exciting parallels for managers and their teams:

- **F1™ is all about winning** – winning races, championships and of course multi-million-dollar sponsorship deals. Winning is the passion that drives F1™ teams. It is talked about all the time and generates passion, excitement and emotion.

> *It's correct that I'm a bad loser. Why should I lie? If I was good at losing I wouldn't be in Formula 1™.*
> Sebastian Vettel[146]

- **Winning in F1™ is clear.** It is marked out on the road in black and white. Everybody knows that it takes 78 laps to complete the 161.734 miles of the Monaco Grand Prix circuit – it can be measured out so there is no doubt.[147] For many organizations the definition of winning is a lot fuzzier. Many managers struggle to define what winning actually means for their organizations, teams and team members.

> *It doesn't matter what the trophy looks like as long as it has '1st' on it!*
> Lewis Hamilton[148]

- In F1™ there is a **shared definition of success** and everybody is working on helping the same cars and drivers to win. However, in organizations, goals, priorities and KPIs set at a functional, project and team level often mean that for one part of the organization to win another must lose.

- **In F1™ winning is celebrated.** It is high profile and glamorous - Champagne, trophies, laurels, and the adulation of fans. Winning drivers are made to feel on top of the world. Yet many organizations are poor at celebrating success or the progress being made along the way. According to Growth Pitstop™ benchmarking data the scope for improvement here is 32%, but it may be considerably higher as many managers think that they are better in this area than they are. Failing to celebrate success or progress represents a lost opportunity for building confidence, motivation and engagement among teams.

If managers embraced the concept of winning the same way as F1™ they could significantly boost their success, while at the same time achieving a new level of engagement among their teams.

> *...the difference between winning and losing is often subjective and open to the vagaries of political interpretation. What aggravates this is a lack of focus on the alignment of goals between stakeholders at the outset of a plan and the regular re-contracting of goals as the plan is implemented.*
> Ian Blakey & John Day[149]

THE DESIRE TO WIN

Most managers have something in common with every F1™ champion. They want to win! The difference is that in F1™ everybody knows where the finishing line is. In organizations, the same does not necessarily apply.   Across a senior management team of six people there could be as many as six different definitions of what winning means. The result is that managers and their teams may be moving at different speeds and perhaps even in different directions.

Has Your Team's Got A Clear:

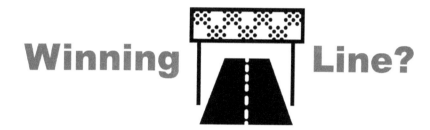

Winning Line?

Harnessing the innate desire to win that exists within managers and their teams can accelerate like nothing else. Yet plans and strategies with their SMART objectives rarely talk about winning. Listen in on any management or team meeting and you won't hear much talk about winning either. Words like 'competition,' 'performance' and 'KPIs' are part of everyday management speak, but 'winning' is not. Yet there is nothing more critical to the performance of an organization, manager, or team. So, before we go any further take a few minutes to reflect on the following questions:

Q: When have _you_ won over the past 6 or 12 months?

_____

_____

Q: When has _your_ organization/ team won over the past 6 or 12 months?

_____

_____

The topic of winning goes to the core of your personal motivation, your values and your strategy. Over the coming pages, we will explore several different perspectives on winning. We invite you to be curious - writing and re-writing your definitions of winning as you read on.

> *...the single most crucial dimension of a company's aspiration: a company must play to win. To play merely to participate is self-defeating. It is a recipe for mediocrity.*
> A.G. Lafley & Roger L. Martin[150]

TALKING ABOUT WINNING

Management and strategy gurus have for a long time emphasized the importance of mission, vision and purpose to the success of an organization. Similarly, motivational speakers and coaches emphasize their importance to the performance of individuals and teams[151]. But while most managers agree with the merit of such goal-setting, they rarely get excited about it. Indeed, the opposite is often the case.

> *A mission statement won't propel a business forward...*
> Richard P. Rumelt[152]

The underlying principle – the need for organizations and teams to know where they are going or what they want to achieve – is as valid as ever. Without it organizations and teams risk pulling in different directions, thereby squandering their energies and resources. Yet most corporate mission statements or visions are little more than poetry – fancy words that read well, but ring hollow. That is because the aspirations of the boardroom bards that write them fail to connect with the troops at the front line, or perhaps even reality on the ground. There is widespread cynicism regarding vision setting (and corporate strategizing more generally). That is because it fails to engage people either intellectually or emotionally.   Thus, the motivation for changing the dialog – to start talking about winning.

Just the word 'winning' alone is powerful and evocative. Why not use it more often among your team? A dialog about winning, including the rewards of winning and the implications of losing, is a powerful change agent especially for teams that are struggling or misaligned. A dialog about winning might include discussing such revealing questions as:

- Are we winning? When? Where?
- What is winning?
- Are we all winning?
- Do we expect / deserve to win?
- Are there areas where winning is proving difficult?
- When do we lose?
- What prevents us from winning?
- What capabilities / resources would enable us to win more?
- What would we do if we believed that we could not fail?

Discussing these questions is core to the process of defining what winning really means.

> *Underlying a true sense of (business) urgency is a set of feelings: a compulsive determination to move, and win, now.*
> J.P. Kotter[153]

Do you have a winning team?   Find out by completing then diagram below. Ask your colleagues to do the same.

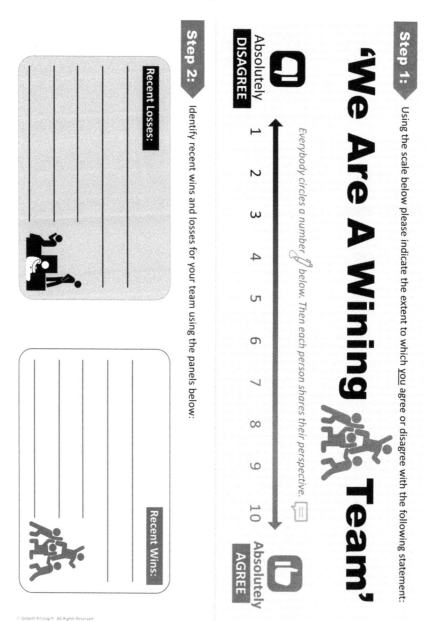

THE 'WHY?' QUESTION

The BIG question at the at the core of the performance debate rarely gets answered. It is the 'Why?' question. Why are we doing it? Why all the hard work, the orders won, products or services delivered, the service calls handled and the payments collected? What drives us to do it today and will drive us to do it again tomorrow, only better? The 'Why?' question is central to the discussion about winning. It was at the center of the performance 'lollipop' – that is the 'in the round view of performance' that includes task, social, decision and development[154].

Managers and teams spend a lot of time talking about and attending to the 'how?' – setting plans, taking-action, and so on. All too often the 'Why?' question is left unanswered. Managers assume that the 'Why' is clear to all – also that it is compelling. They are often shocked and surprised (even annoyed) when they hear that it is not. If there is one key warning from all our performance analytics and behavioral analysis it is: don't assume the 'Why?' behind any of your organization/team's key priorities, strategies or initiatives is clear to all those involved. Moreover, even if it is clear today, don't assume that it won't become muddled and confused over the next 3, 6 or 9 months. So, begin every planning or review meeting by asking the simple question 'why are we doing this?' Reaffirming and clarifying the 'why?' is a great place to start as well as to end any important team meeting or workshop.

> *In business, we tend to obsess over the "how"—as in "Here's how to do it." Yet we rarely discuss the "why"—as in "Here's why we're doing it." But it's often difficult to do something exceptionally well if we don't know the reasons we're doing it in the first place.*
> Neel Doshi & Lindsay McGrego[155]

DEFINING WHAT WINNING MEANS

As we have said, in F1™ the finish line for every race is clearly marked out. The requirements of winning are clear in terms of number of laps and lap times. Not so in business. To understand what winning really means for your organization requires exploring three dimensions – shown in the table.

Dimension	Defining Winning
3 **Time horizons**	Winning in the short-term, medium-term and longer-term (3, 12 and 24 months).
3 **Perspectives**	What 'winning' means for you, your organization and your team.
3 **Levels** of winning	Winning that is defined in terms of finances, strategies and / or passions.

By exploring these three dimensions you will be guided to a definition of winning that has the maximum prospect of being realized because it balances the short-term with the longer-term, financial and more strategic or meaningful goals, as well as personal and team goals. Think of it as a 3D view of winning.

Winning in 3D

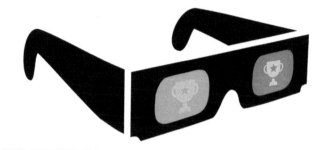

3 Horizons - 3 Perspectives - 3 Levels

THREE TIME HORIZONS FOR WINNING

In F1™ it is easy to break success down into its many steps – the time trials, laps and race circuits that are required. So, while teams have a single overall goal for winning, it is broken down into many smaller goals. This enables progress to be tracked and provides the encouragement and confidence that comes from the accumulation of many smaller wins. Managers must simultaneously manage three horizons of growth[156] – short-term, medium-term and long-term. That means winning today, tomorrow and into the future. With this in mind, reflect on what winning looks like over time by completing the panels overleaf.

WINNING: 3 Time Horizons

Define winning for your team across the 3 time horizons below:

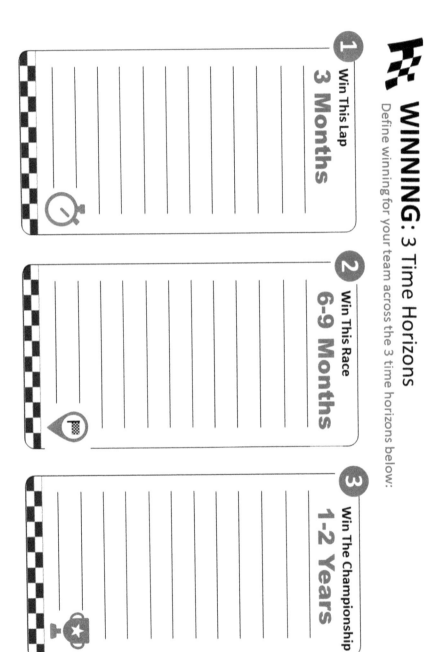

1 Win This Lap
3 Months

2 Win This Race
6-9 Months

3 Win The Championship
1-2 Years

Link short-term realities to long-term dreams. Hound yourself and others with questions about what it takes to link the never-ending now to the sweet dreams you hope to realize later.
Hayagreeva Rao & Robert I. Sutton[157]

THREE PERSPECTIVES ON WINNING

Managers tend to assume that everybody on their team knows what the goal, vision or strategy is. Then they get frustrated when people express confusion or doubt. Rarely do managers pause to consider whether others are fired up by or committed to the goals or strategies that have been set. That is a problem because our benchmarking data shows that, while 75% say that there is a clear vision for the future of the business, only 46% are fired up by it. Moreover, the further one moves from the C-suite the less fired-up people seem to become.

3 perspectives on **winning**:

YOU   YOUR **TEAM**   YOUR **ORG.**

When it comes to winning within organizations, more than one perspective is required. It is not just the ambition of the CEO or the senior management team that matters. The challenge is to ensure that the ambition of those below is equal to, if not greater than, those above. Moreover, it is to ensure that the ambitions of all are aligned towards the achievement of a singular vision of success. That requires three perspectives on winning – yours, your team's and your organization's. Let's explore each of these in turn.

(a) Getting Personal about Winning

F1™ champions are incredibly ambitious. You have to be determined to succeed in order to make it into such an exclusive club – it has only about 20 drivers. In organizations (as in F1™) everybody wants to win – they want to succeed. The only problem is that what winning means varies greatly.

Psychologists tell us that you cannot understand human behavior without addressing its underlying motivations and ambitions. A person's definition of winning reveals where they are focused and what they are aiming for, as well as their level of ambition, confidence and motivation. It is also about their happiness and well-being. When you ask people to define winning you will find there is a personal dimension to winning that goes beyond business success.

> *Superbosses have mastered something most bosses miss—a path to extraordinary success founded on making other people successful.*
> Sydney Finkelstein[158]

Ask your team members what winning means to them personally and here is what you are likely to hear:

- Job and financial security.

- Career progression.
- A nice place to work, a good atmosphere.
- Doing work that I enjoy.
- Acknowledgment – recognition by the public / peers.
- Savings – getting married and moving to a new house.
- Stress – not to be continually fighting fires.
- Being part of a team.
- Clear sense of purpose – know I am making progress.
- Learning new things / developing new skills / mastery.
- Respect – being valued and appreciated.
- Doing something worthwhile (helping others / leaving the world a better place).
- Work-life balance - taking weekends and evenings off. Time with my family
- Building or creating something – leaving a legacy – giving something back.

What we do in our organizations should be a logical expression of our desire to win, both personal and professional. A manager must know what winning means for each member of his or team and to ensure that the goals of the business connect, rather than compete, with these definitions of winning.

> *... managers need to think not only about what's best for their own firms, but also about how what they do affects others.*
>
> Cynthia Montgomery[159]

Your definition of winning is akin to finding 'true north' – that is the point by which you and your team can navigate to success. 'Without it', as one of our coaches says, 'how will you know if you have gone off course?' Finding out what winning means is key to understanding what motivates you. But it can require some digging however, as what we publicly espouse as our winning objectives can be at variance with our deeper motivations and drive to win. Furthermore, tied up in the day-to-day, managers often lose sight of the bigger picture – the bigger prize.

Playing to Win?

Some people are 'playing to win', while others 'playing not to lose'[160]. That is to say; there are two dominant motivations:

- **Not Losing**: To <u>protect</u> what they already have, maintain the status quo, or to prevent / avoid something happening.

- **Winning**: The prospect of achieving a goal, or otherwise making <u>progress</u>.

Using the table overleaf, take 30 minutes to write what winning and not losing means for you, or your team.

(b) Team Perspectives on Winning

While it is the driver that gets most attention, **winning in F1™ requires a team effort.** The tag line on F1™ champion Lewis Hamilton's website says it all: "We win and lose together." Even drivers with the biggest of egos know that they owe their success to their cars and those who build and maintain them. All this means that there MUST be a shared definition of winning. Finding out what winning means to the different members of your management team is very important.

> *Few, if any, forces in human affairs are as powerful as shared vision.*
> Peter M. Senge[161]

There are two ways of defining your motivation/goals. Use both by filling the panels below:

❶ WINNING

The Progress / Achievements You Want:

Job & Career Ambition:

Relationships & Family:

Finances & Wealth:

Friends & Social:

Activities & Leisure:

Health & Well-being:

Other:

❷ Not LOSING

What you want to Protect / Maintain / Avoid:

Job & Career:

Relationships & Family:

Finances & Wealth:

Friends & Social:

Activities & Leisure:

Health & Well-being:

Other:

CONFIDENTIAL

People must find their own meaning and purpose - it cannot simply be handed to them. Anything that has been written on strategy in the past decade is very clear on this point – the notion of the vision or strategy set by a select few at the top of the organization and then communicated to the suppliant masses is a recipe for failure.

What Motivates Your People? As a manager do you know what motivates your team? In the picture team members define what winning means for them, as well as for their organization. It is a powerful way of generating a debate about winning and igniting people's passions (see end of this section).

You need great passion because everything you do with great pleasure you do well.
Juan Manuel Fangio, racing champion[162]

(c) Winning for the Organization

Managers tend to equate growth and performance with winning, as in the Growth Pitstop™ below where the checkered flag and the upward graph are intertwined. But for many organizations and teams, performance or growth doesn't necessarily mean winning. Indeed, it could mean the opposite and when this happens growth inevitably suffers as a result. An organization cannot succeed in the long-term, if its definition of winning is at odds with what winning means for the members of its team.

The first step in fueling your team's ambition is to define what success actually means for you and your team. This will enable you to explore whether it is possible for you to win and for your team to win at the same time. It requires setting your goals in a way that ensures the following holds true:

Performance = Winning

To understand why this equation matters, complete the from overleaf identifying what winning means for you, your team and your organization.

> *Nothing else is more important to the survival and success of a firm than why it exists, and what otherwise unmet needs it intends to fill.*
> Cynthia Montgomery[163]

WINNING: 3 Perspectives

Define winning for You, Your Team and Your Organization below:

1 Winning for
ME

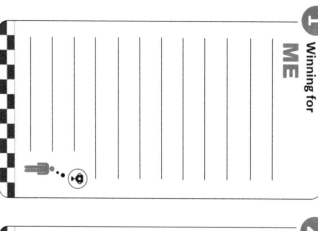

2 Winning for
TEAM

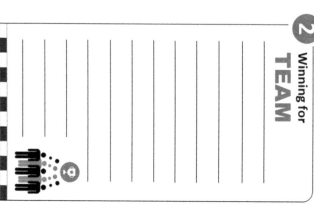

3 Winning for
ORG.

THREE LEVELS OF WINNING

Winning on the racetrack means getting the car across the line ahead of the competition. The expression 'winning by a nose' has particular relevance as it is the nose cone of the car that must cross the finishing line in order to win. In exploring the power of winning ambition, we look at the nose cone as having three levels – as shown in the diagram.

3 Levels of Winning

Winning in F1™ requires going faster. But does winning for your organization or team mean performing better, or indeed growing faster? The answer depends on what type of growth (or winning) it is:

Level 1 Winning: Involves the key performance metrics of your organization, or team. It may be those essential business metrics - **sales, profit or cash** – that keep the shareholders (and other stakeholders) happy and the bills paid. Alternatively, it may include other metrics relating to output, quality, efficiency, satisfaction, or anything else that measures performance. This level 1 winning typically involves a short-term focus on financial, or related results.

Level 2 Winning: To sustain performance organizations must execute on key projects, priorities and **strategies that will enable them to win into the future**. These promise a greater future dividend and cannot be measured by reference to short term results (i.e. level 1 winning). They are aimed at developing the team's ability to win today and win tomorrow. In this way Level 2 winning focuses on the requirements of delivering and sustaining performance. It is similar to a balanced scorecard that goes beyond the financial numbers, to include operational measures relating to the strategy of the organization[164]. It is a view of performance 'in the round' that includes; task effectiveness, social health, decision smarts and development potential[165].

> *Once something is a passion the motivation is there...*
> Michael Schumacher[166]

Level 3 Winning: Fueling performance requires **igniting passions**. An ambition for a type of dream-chasing or self-actualizing growth is found at Level 3. There is a temptation to view this type of ambition or goal as being less hard-nosed, or perhaps even soft. Yet they are as powerful, if not more powerful, a lever of performance and potential than any other goal.

> *If a person has no dreams, they no longer have any reason to live. Dreaming is necessary, although in the dream reality should be glimpsed. For me this is a principle of life...*
> Ayrton Senna[167]

Level 1 winning is what you read about in an organization's financial reports, KPIs and metrics. But rarely is that enough to separate the fast and the best from the rest. It is unlikely that the targets your organization has set define the limits of your team's ambition. The different levels of winning, or definitions of performance and growth, are summarized in the next table.

The Three Levels of Winning:

Level 1: Performance	Level 2: Priorities (Key Plans, Projects & Strategies)	Level 3: Passions
Sales-winning Profit-generating Cash-spinning Return on Capital EBIDTA Dividends Output Efficiency	Maximizing Potential Value-creating (for customers / channels) Obstacle-overcoming Competence-building Innovation Boundary-expanding (new products / markets) Competitive advantage-building / sustaining	People Purpose Passion-igniting Sustainable Ethical Benevolent Visionary Inspirational

> *Companies want to launch new products, grow their market share, and expand into new markets; employees want to take on new responsibilities, increase their capabilities, and yes, make more money. In other words, both company and employee want to be on a winning team.*
>
> Reid Hoffman and Ben Casnocha[168]

While most managers have heard of Maslow's Hierarchy of Needs, those who define winning in terms of meeting financial targets, have cut the top off the pyramid (as in the next diagram).[169]

They assume that their organizations, managers and teams are 'coin-operated' – primarily motivated by money. As a result, the approach to motivation within many organizations fails to address as many as three out of five of the factors that motivate people to high levels of performance.[170]

> I talk to a lot of CEOs, and everyone professes a commitment to building a "high performance" organization—but is this really possible when the core values of the corporation are venal rather than transcendent? I don't think so.
> Garry Hammel[171]

The purpose of the business may still be to execute strategies that maximize profit and shareholder value, but there is a big difference between purpose and passion. It is only the latter that fuels people. Money is very important, but it is not everything. Is another 10% or 20% more money going to impact on the behavior or the passion of Lewis Hamilton? Would Schumacher have achieved the same success even if he earned 20%, 30% or even 50% less?

It is going to be difficult for your organization to be in first place if it only uses third rate goals to motivate its people. So, listen to what really motivates your people. The level of your team's winning ambition will determine the level of your team's commitment. For example, if winning is defined in terms of organizational revenue and profit (level 1 winning) you are likely to get only level 1 commitment.

> *Teams win when their individual members trust each other enough to prioritize team success over individual glory; paradoxically, winning as a team is the best way for the team members to achieve individual success.*
> Reid Hoffman and Ben Casnocha[172]

Once people are free of the worry of having enough money to meet their basic needs (and a little more besides) they are free to move up towards the pinnacle of the nose cone, just like in Maslow's hierarchy. As one normally hard-nosed manager participating in a Performance Pitstop put it; 'winning sounds hollow when it is just a number'. Money alone can't accelerate your organization the way that passion can.

> *The moment money becomes your motivation you are immediately not as good as someone who is stimulated by PASSION and INTERNAL WILL.*
> Sebastian Vettel[173]

Explore the 3 Levels of winning for your organization/team by completing the panels in the diagram overleaf.

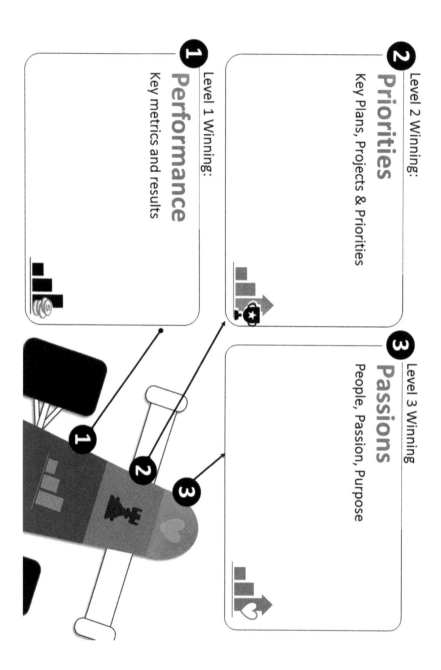

Level 2 Winning:
Priorities
Key Plans, Projects & Priorities

Level 1 Winning:
Performance
Key metrics and results

Level 3 Winning
Passions
People, Passion, Purpose

YOUR WINNING LINE TEST

In racing winning is very clear. It is painted in black and white at the end of the racetrack. In this exercise bring your team together to define what winning is by creating an actual finishing/winning line. This exercise will get people's imaginations going and generate a searching discussion about what really motivates people in their work. Here are the steps:

1. Give each person one white and one black sheet (of A4 paper or card) to define what winning is this year (or next year if you are near year-end).

2. On the black sheet draw or write **what winning means for <u>us as a team</u>**, using a white marker, or chalk.

3. On the white sheet draw or write what winning means for you in connection with your job.

3. Doodle, draw and scribble to make your sheets as personalized as possible – doing this will connect

with your creativity, as well as your emotions.

4. When everybody is finished arranging the black and white cards on the floor to form the **chequered winning line**. It might look like the image on the previous page.

5. Let the **discussion** begin. Ask each person to share with the group how they defined winning. Probe by asking people to reflect a little more about what they have written or drawn means and why it matters to them.

6. When everybody has finished, ask people to reflect on what, if anything the discussion has **revealed**. You might like to ask questions such as:

- Is winning for us as a group clear?

- Do we all have the same definition of winning?

- How well do we know what winning means for other team members?

- How will we know when winning has happened?

- How well do we celebrate winning?

6. Tape your finishing line together and put it somewhere that it will serve to continually focus your team on winning.

Extraordinary groups exhibit... a compelling purpose that inspires and stretches members to make the group and its work a top priority.
Geoffrey M. Bellman & Kathleen D. Ryan[174]

Just as race-car drivers keep their eyes fixed on the road ahead, creators focus on the future, knowing that where they go, their eyes go first.
Amy Wilkinson[175]

Building the Pitstop Winning Line

In the picture pitstop conference attendees build the winning line. It is a powerful exercise aimed at exploring what motivates the members of a team.

The result is a definition of success for the individual and the organization - one that goes far beyond the typical mission statement or corporate vision.

All change, even very large and powerful change, begins when a few people start talking with one another about something they care about.
Margaret J. Wheatley[176]

A racing car has only ONE objective: to WIN motor races. If it does not do this it is nothing but a waste of time, money, and effort.
Colin Chapman, Lotus F1™ team founder[177]

WANT MORE? SHOP ONLINE

Now that you have read the book, what's next? Go online to find a range of Pitstop to Perform™ products to support you on your performance journey, including:

Workshop Kits

Everything you need to run a pitstop workshop with your team in one box.

Pitstop Posters

Keep the Pitstop Meta-model™ front of mind with posters for your office.

Pitstop Analytics™

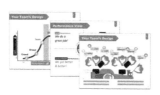

Assess the performance potential of your team using Pitstop Analytics™.

Research Insights

Access insights & tools on any part of the meta-model (e.g Right People).

Shop online at: www.GrowthPitstop.com/shop

PITSTOP KIT

Here are some of the tools that you are likely to need in a pitstop conference or program.

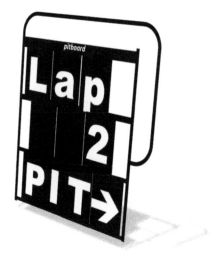

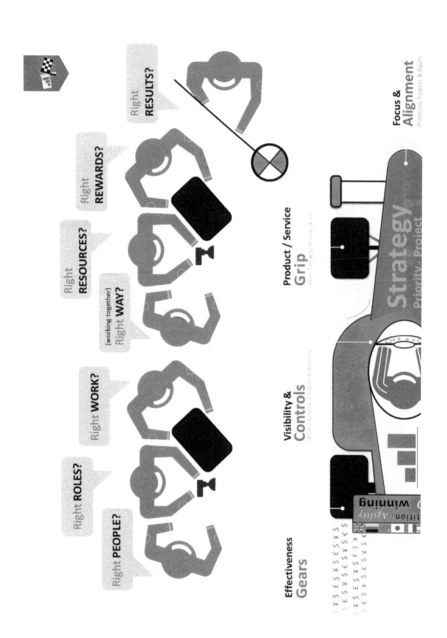

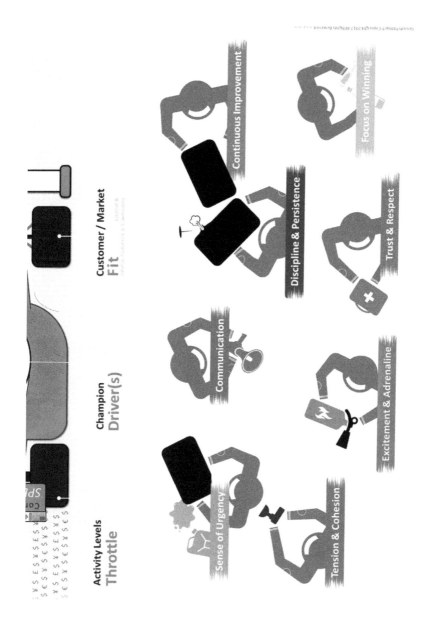

1 Why do you feel it **needs to improve**?

> [   ]

2 On a scale of 1 to 10, where 1 = very low & 10 = very high

(a) How you **rate**
this area today: [/10   ]

(b) You'd like to
increase it to: [/10   ]

3 What does success look like **for you** (& how will you measure it)?

> [   ]

4 What **benefits** do you expect?

> [   ]

5 What % **impact do you think it** could
have on revenue in a year? [%   ]

6 How **important** is this?

(a)

Is this likely
to be a **top 3**
priority for you?

Yes ☐
No ☐
Don't ☐
Know

(b)

Will it really
matter to your
manager/CEO?

Yes ☐
No ☐
Don't ☐
Know

7 How **confident** are you of success?

On a scale of 1 to 10, where 1 = very low & 10 = very high

/10

8 What could **stop** you improving it?

9 What time & resources will it require?

10 What help or input will you need?

Name: _____   Date: _____

Where ✈ Is Your Team?

Put your team or business unit on the grid below.
Then discuss with your peers.

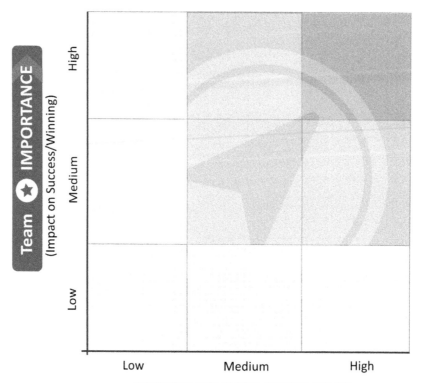

Team ⭐ IMPORTANCE
(Impact on Success/Winning)

High

Medium

Low

Low   Medium   High

Team ⚙ PERFORMANCE

(Effectiveness)

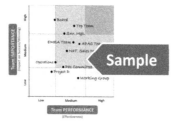

1 What do you **like** about being on this team?

_____

_____

_____

_____

2 What are your **strengths** as a team member?

_____

_____

_____

_____

3 What are you **learning** from being on this team?

_____

_____

_____

_____

4 What are your **deltas** (areas for development) as a team member?

_____

_____

_____

_____

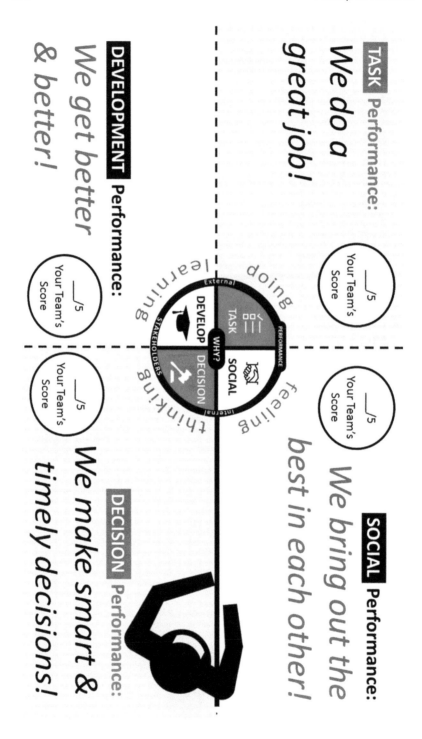

TASK Performance:

We do a great job!

Your Team's Score ___/5

SOCIAL Performance:

We bring out the best in each other!

Your Team's Score ___/5

DEVELOPMENT Performance:

We get better & better!

Your Team's Score ___/5

DECISION Performance:

We make smart & timely decisions!

Your Team's Score ___/5

SOCIAL Performance:
We bring out the best in each other!

2.1 Affinity for Team
2.2 Shared Values/Purpose
2.3 Positive Interactions
2.4 Supportive Relationships
2.5 Conducive Environment
2.6 Limited 'Us Vs Them'

DECISION Performance:
We are clever and wise!

3.1 Time to Think
3.2 Accurate View of Reality
3.3 Exploration of Alternatives
3.4 Creative Problem Solving
3.5 Avoidance of Groupthink
3.6 Decision Making Autonomy

TASK Performance:
We get the job done!

1.1 Meaningful Work
1.2 Performance Ethos
1.3 Mutual Accountability
1.4 Synergistic Interdependence
1.5 Team Reflexivity
1.6 Winning Momentum

DEVELOP Potential:
We strive for better & better!

4.1 Belief in Team & Team Members
4.2 Ability to envision a better future
4.3 Desire to Learn / Develop / Grow
4.4 Culture of No Blaming & No Hiding
4.5 Curiosity & Experimentation
4.6 Investment in Learning & Innovation

Internal

STAKEHOLDERS

SOCIAL

WHY?

DECISION

TASK

DEVELOP

STAKEHOLDERS

External

ECONOMIC Well-being:

Fair & equitable pay & financial stability

PSYCHOLOGICAL Well-being:

Thriving as a 'whole person'

SOCIAL Well-being:

Affinity & belonging, Friendship & support

PHYSICAL Well-being:

Ensure safety, promote health & optimize the workplace

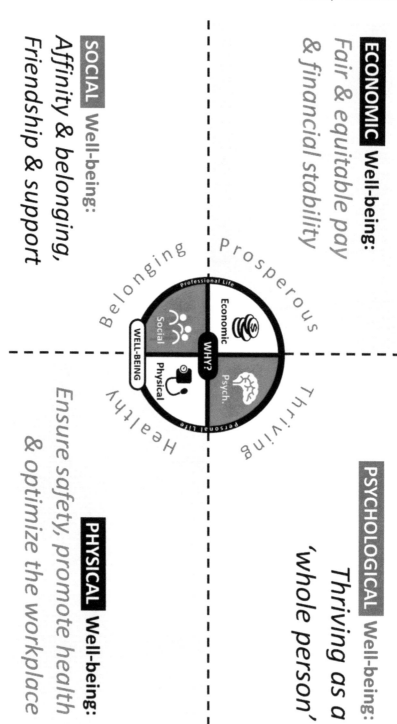

Task-Related Norms

To get our work done effectively as a team:

We should:

We should avoid:

Social / Group Norms*

To develop a healthy team that we all want to belong to:

We should:

We should avoid:

Out-of-Bounds Behavior

When a team violates team norms :

We should:

We should avoid:

Less Of:

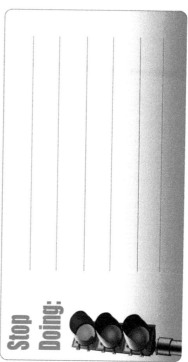

Stop
Doing:

MORE OF:

- Problem/Opportunity Definition Mode - Area worked on: _____

Pitlane No:

1 'As Is'

Describe the situation
as it is today

2 'To Be'

Describe the situation as it is should
be or what we want to achieve

- Solutions Mode -   Area worked on: _____   Pitlane No:

3

Company

Describe what
management
can do

4

Ourselves

Describe what
you & your team
can/will do

Awareness Checker

Step 1: Circle the emotions you witnessed. Circle repeatedly if they resurfaced.
Step 2: Put a 'e' beside the moods or emotions you personally experienced.
Step 3: Dialogue with your coach or team.

Quiet Positive
Calm
Content
Relaxed
Relieved
Serene

Positive & Lively
Amusement
Delight
Elation
Excitement
Happiness
Joy
Pleasure

Positive Thoughts
Courage
Hope
Pride
Satisfaction
Trust

Caring
Affection
Empathy
Friendliness
Love

Agitation
Stress
Shock
Tension

Reactive
Interest
Politeness
Surprised

Negative Thoughts
Doubt
Envy
Frustration
Guilt
Shame

Negative & Not in Control
Anxiety
Fear
Lonely
Embarrassment
Helplessness
Powerlessness
Worry

Negative & Passive
Boredom
Despair
Disappointment
Hurt
Sadness

Negative & Forceful
Anger
Annoyance
Contempt
Disgust
Irritation

Inventory of emotions as compiled by the Human-Machine Interaction Network on Emotion (HUMAINE).

PitLane Change Model

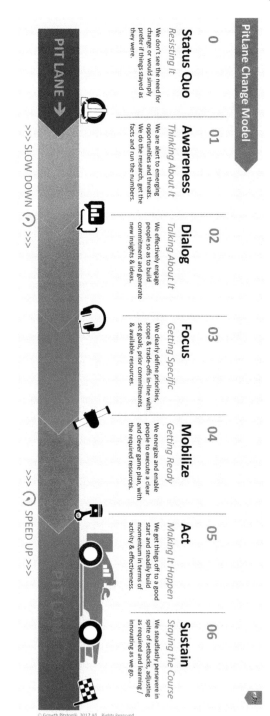

PIT LANE →

>>> SLOW DOWN ◔ >>>   >>> ◔ SPEED UP >>>

0

Status Quo
Resisting It

We don't see the need for change or would simply prefer if things stayed as they were.

01

Awareness
Thinking About It

We are alert to emerging opportunities and threats. We do the research, get the facts and run the numbers.

02

Dialog
Talking About It

We effectively engage people so as to build commitment and generate new insights & ideas.

03

Focus
Getting Specific

We clearly define priorities, scope & trade-offs in-line with set goals, prior commitments & available resources.

04

Mobilize
Getting Ready

We energize and enable people to execute a clear and clever game plan, with the required resources.

05

Act
Making It Happen

We get things off to a good start and steadily build momentum in terms of activity & effectiveness.

06

Sustain
Staying the Course

We steadfastly persevere in spite of setbacks, adjusting as required and learning / innovating as we go.

Your Team's Pit Score

Circle the number that best describes your team's performance at its last important meeting and then add up all of the scores.

	Scale		
Poor trust	1 2 3 4 5		High Trust
Poor Communication	1 2 3 4 5		Good Communication
Poor Focus	1 2 3 4 5		Clear Focus
No Urgency	1 2 3 4 5		Maximum Urgency
Low Energy Levels	1 2 3 4 5		High Energy Levels
Poor Teamwork	1 2 3 4 5		Great Teamwork
No Passion Evident	1 2 3 4 5		Passion Highly Evident
Winning doesn't matter	1 2 3 4 5		It's all about winning
Indecisive	1 2 3 4 5		Decisive
Confused Roles	1 2 3 4 5		Clear Roles
Fear	1 2 3 4 5		Courage
Old thinking/Solutions	1 2 3 4 5		Creative Problem Solving

Source: Ray Collis & John O Gorman, 'Growth Pitstop', ASG Press, 2016.

Step 1: Calculate your score (Max score 12 * 5 = 60): _____

Step 2: Deduct one point for every time you witnessed:

- People shouting over each other.
- People not waiting for others to finish their sentences.
- People who were missing, arrived late or left early.
- People checking phones or other devices.

- Each person who tried to dominate the meeting.

- Each person who contributed little, if at all to the meeting.

- Every time somebody pointed the finger of blame at another individual or group.

- Every undiscussable or 'elephant in the room' missing from the discussion.

Step 3: Add one point for:

- Every respectful challenge.

- Every element of constructive feedback or encouragement.

- Anytime a person said they 'got it wrong', 'it's not working' or 'let's try another approach'.

- Every function, team or business that was represented or at least whose perspective is reflected.

Step 4: Calculate final score: _____

Step 5: Now check your score:

55+	Mercedes™ or Red Bull™ want your pit team!
45 - 55	Very close to becoming high-performing pit team.
36 - 45	Pit team in waiting – team development needed.
25 - 35	You have a group rather than a team in the pit lane.
<25	Your team is 'the pits' (urban slang for very poor).

APPENDICES

- Performance Analytics
- Pitstop Programs
- Research Methodology
- The Growth Pitstop Organization
- About the Authors
- Other Books in the Pitstop Series

PERFORMANCE ANALYTICS

What gets measured, gets managed. But how do you measure performance potential?

It is vital to bring objective analysis and external measurement to any questions of performance. That includes design, dynamics, leadership, strategy and execution. This is the role of Pitstop Analytics™ - a cutting-edge Predictive Performance Analytics solution from Growth Pitstop™ and the core technology around which the concepts and models in this book were developed.

Data-Driven Performance Decisions

This book provides an insight into the pitstop meta-model, specifically the 7 design factors and 8 dynamics at the top and bottom of the model. However, the full meta-model encompasses 186 variables, including:

• Alignment	• Talent Development	• Decision Smarts
• Culture	• Org./Team Structure	• Engagement
• Leadership	• Psychological Safety	• Commitment
• Execution	• Task Effectiveness	• Well-being
• Teamwork	• Return on Collaboration	• Group Dynamics

Big Data for Performance

Inspired by the use of BIG data to drive performance in F1™, the PitStop Analytics™ platform scientifically measures performance and potential within organizations, business units, teams, and individuals. It enables data-driven decisions in respect of talent, alignment, purpose, structure, strategy-execution, teamwork and culture.

Data gathering is cloud-based and takes just 26 mins per person. Once the data is gathered algorithms and predictive models take over.

Data-driven Decisions

Throughout this book you are asked to make assessments regarding your team's performance potential, its Zone of Performance and the performance losses keeping it there. But how confident are you in the accuracy of your answers?

Pistop Analytics™ will enable you to:

- **Scientifically assess** the performance potential of your organization, business unit or team, specifically its P2P Metric™.
- **Systematically exploit** the next 5%, 10%, 15% or your organization, business unit or team's full potential – called Performance Gains.
- **Identify & tackle** those Performance Losses preventing your team spending more time in the Zone of Peak Performance™.

The P2P Metric™ is the ratio of performance to potential for an organization, business unit or team. As examined in Section 2 it is a yardstick against which performance potential can be measured, adjusted and monitored over time – one that enables internal and external comparison too.

Predictive Performance Analytics

An accurate diagnosis is key to understanding performance. But looking back at what has happened is not enough – looking to the future is essential. Pitstop Analytics™ combines powerful diagnostics with predictive modelling, thereby providing insight to both present and future performance.

Powerful Data Visualization

Pitstop to Perform™ analytics extract meaning from masses of data by modelling and predicting performance – just like in F1™. Using the pitstop meta-model the data is brought to life and tells a story. Users can visualize their performance data in an intuitive manner – patterns and trends are automatically recognized, and attention drawn to performance alerts, blind-spots, and contradictions. Thus, data is transformed into actionable insight.

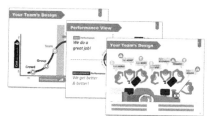

Access the analytics or find out more at:
www.growthpitstop.com/analytics or email:
support@growthpitstop.com.

PITSTOP PROGRAMS

Planning a Leadership Program or Growth Initiative?

Movement is at the heart of the Pitstop process, hence the model (below) has a triangular shape – reflective of the delta symbol - the icon for change.

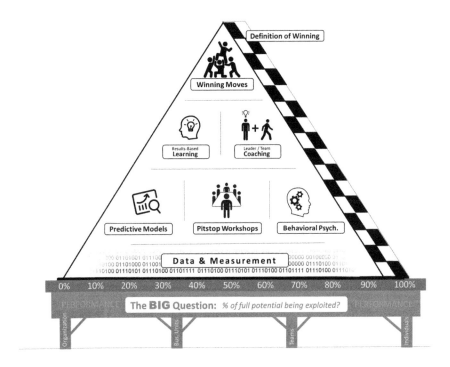

PitStop to Perform™ programs are customized to span 3, 6 or 12 months and consist of the 8 key elements summarized overleaf.

1. Performance Data

Inspired by the use of BIG data to drive performance in F1™, the PitStop Analytics platform scientifically measures performance and potential within organizations, business units, teams, and individuals. It captures 186  performance variables to enable data-driven decisions in the areas of data driven decision in respect of talent, alignment, purpose, structure, strategy-execution, teamwork and culture.

Data gathering is cloud-based and takes just 26 mins per person. Once the data is gathered algorithms and predictive models take over systematically scanning for performance losses, risks, and gains – measuring, categorizing, and prioritizing them.

2. Predictive Performance Analytics

Pitstop to Perform™ analytics extract meaning from masses of data by modelling and predicting performance – just like in F1™. Using the pitstop meta-model the data is brought to life and tells a story.

Users can visualize their performance data in an intuitive manner – patterns and trends are recognized automatically, and attention drawn to performance alerts, blind-spots, and contradictions. Thus, data is transformed into actionable insight – pointing leaders and their teams to key winning moves that will transform performance losses into gains.

3. Definition of Winning - Tests of Alignment

Pitstop programs are infused with a passion for winning, just like F1™. They look beyond mission statements and goals, to connect leaders and their teams with a compelling definition of winning that fuels both purpose and passion.

Programs test levels of organization and team ambition, as well as alignment in terms of purpose, priorities, and results. A key objective is a renewed sense of forward momentum, as well as potency and resilience for the team.

4. Winning Moves – Test of Execution

Pitstop programs are about movement and winning. Individuals working alone and in teams will exploit specific performance gains and tackle identified performance losses (as highlighted by the data). Examples include; advancing a key  business priority, improving some aspect of team functioning, or tackling a cumbersome work process. These 'Winning Moves' are the practical means by which quantifiable performance gains will be realized.

In addition to being tests of execution, Winning Moves are also aimed at building execution capacity, as well as confidence and resilience.

5. Behavioral Psychology

There is a psychology to performance – that is to say attitudes and behaviors play an important role. So, too do the dynamics within a group or team including its culture and norms. An organization or team is a complex social system  and the process of change requires engaging with (and respectfully challenging) embedded patterns of behavior. To do this pitstop programs leverage the latest insights from the fields of social psychology and behavioral economics, including Growth Mindset, Psychological Safety and Psychological Well-being[178].

Cognitive Re-reframing, Mental Modelling and Systems Thinking are key to the effectiveness of the pitstop process. So too is the unique 6-step Pitlane Engage-Change Model used to engage teams in the process of change.

6. Pitstop Workshops

Pitstop workshops bring executives, groups and teams together to focus on their own performance opportunities and challenges with a renewed level of energy and engagement. Your team(s) will work as a pit crew. The idea is just like in racing – to come together as a team, identify problems and fix them fast!

Pitstops are simulations of the 'real team' in action and involve a series of exercises to test and build levels of task effectiveness, decision smarts and social health/cohesion. They are also the basis for a structured process of behavioural observation by leaders of their teams.

7. Leader & Team Coaching

Starting something is easy, however keeping it going is often not. PitStop coaching will help sustain the momentum behind the process of change and 'Winning Move' movement. The role of the PitStop coach is to support (as well as  to respectfully challenge) the leader while individuals and the team clarify Winning Moves, review progress and learn from success, obstacles or set-backs. In addition, the coach guides the leader through the effective use of the performance data generated by Pitstop Analytics™, behavioural observation of the team and self-analysis (of personal performance design and dynamics).

8. Results-Based Learning

In a pitstop there is little time for theory and discussion. Action is required and fast learning too - that is why Pitstop programs employ Results-Based Learning™ (RBL). This involves individuals working in small groups on their own  priorities to achieve specific measurable results while growing in confidence and learning through the process. Team members are provided access to results-based learning modules (22 in total) and toolkits to support their Winning Moves and personal/career development.

Find out more at www.growthpitstop.com or contact us by email at: support@growthpitstop.com.

WANT MORE? SHOP ONLINE

Now that you have read the book, what's next? Go online to find a range of Pitstop to Perform™ products to support you on your performance journey, including:

Pitstop Analytics™

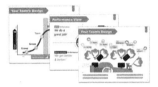

Assess the performance potential of your team using Pitstop Analytics™.

Pitstop Posters

Keep the Pitstop Meta-model™ front of mind with posters for your office.

Workshop Kits

Everything you need to run a pitstop workshop with your team in one box.

Research Insights

Access insights & tools on any part of the meta-model (e.g Right People).

Shop online at: **www.GrowthPitstop.com/shop**

RESEARCH METHDOLOGY

This book is the culmination of ten years of applied research and joint creation with over 3,500 executives from teams and business units within organizations, such as; Great West Life Co., GE, IBM, 3M and Pfizer.

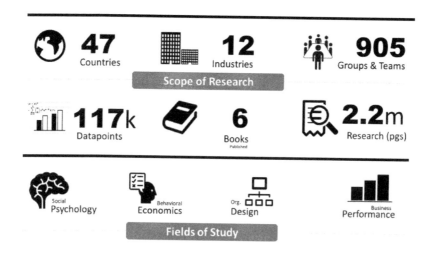

RESEARCH PROGRAM JOURNEY

It's been a major research project spanning over 10 years but also a labor of love. With every team we have worked with we have become even more passionate about the performance and potential of individuals, teams and organizations. This book, along the others in the series, shares that passion with you.

PRIMARY RESEARCH

The primary research involved 900+ groups and teams at all stages of development across 12 industries and 47 markets. These teams were composed of managers and executives from a wide variety of professional backgrounds (including scientists, engineers, accountants, doctors and lawyers).

MULTI-DISCIPLINARY RESEARCH

We have integrated tools and methods from the following fields of study; social psychology, behavioral economics, organizational design and business management. This is a unique blend and it is something that we are particularly proud of.

It is rare to see these 4 categories brought together. Each of these areas, has of itself, generated thousands of pages of research and has its own experts, terminology and publications that present a particular take on the world of performance. But standing alone any of these areas does not present a full picture. It is only when the 4 areas are combined that the complete story of performance can be told. The result is a holistic view of team performance and potential.

THE 'PITSTOP ORGANIZATION'

OUR ORGANIZATION

Pitstop to Perform™ is a product of the Growth Pitstop® organization. We are a new breed of performance solutions provider leveraging data analytics, predictive modelling and behavioral psychology to realize performance gains of 7-25% within organizations, business units, leaders and teams.

Growth PitStop ™

Growth Pitstop® has a growing international network of development, delivery and client partners.

OUR SERVICES

Pitstop to Perform™ is at the core of a range of products and services we offer for senior leaders and their teams, including:

- Performance Analytics (see Appendix)

- Leadership Programs (see Appendix)

- Team-building & Alignment Events

- Training in the areas of performance and growth

- Conferences and Away-days

In addition to our expertise in the area of organization and team performance, we have a deep specialty in terms of the cross-functional requirements of growth, as well as the success of the revenue generating functions of the organization.

OUR WORK

Growth Pitstop® works with ambitious organisations and teams operating in high pressure competitive environments and faced with an accelerated pace of technological, legislative or other change. Example clients include business units and teams within Pfizer, GE, 3M, BT, Great West Life Co. and IBM.

Inspired by the performance obsessed field of F1™ racing, we help leaders and their teams to win - that is winning on 3 levels; organizational, team and individual.

Growth Pitstop® helps leaders, business units and teams to spend as much time as possible in the Zone of Peak Performance™ using a systematic model and process that transforms performance losses into measurable gains. It also focuses those factors essential to sustained performance, including psychological safety, organization/team affinity and well-being.

OUR INNOVATION

Growth Pitstop® has been pioneering research in the areas of performance and growth for over a decade. In addition to 6 published books we have pioneered new innovations in meta-modelling, predictive analytics and the psychology of performance.

Pitstop to Perform™ is the first in the world to integrate behavioural dynamics and organizational/team design with business strategy and execution. It is also the first to transform performance losses into measurable gains.

OUR COMMUNITY

Interested in joining our community? Interested in joining our partner or client community? Please email us at:

support@growthpitstop.com.

ABOUT THE AUTHORS

This book and the meta-model at its core are the creation of thousands of managers and 900+ teams across 12 industries and 47 markets. However, as there are too many people to name, it is the names of Ray Collis (Oslo) and John O' Gorman (Dublin) that appear on the cover. This is their sixth book.

John O' Gorman is an accredited executive coach and managing partner of Growth PitStop®. His passion is performance psychology, unlocking human potential and aligning models of growth and performance thinking. John holds a first-class honors International MBA, Bachelor of Commerce Degree and Diplomas in Marketing and Executive Coaching.

Ray Collis lives in Oslo (Norway) leads the development of the Growth Pitstop®'s cloud-based data analytics and algorithm, now used to identify millions of dollars of performance losses and potential gains across the financial services, pharmaceutical, medical device and high-tech sectors. Ray holds Masters and Bachelor's degrees in Business.

To contact John and Ray or the Growth Pitstop® Community please email: support@growthpitstop.com.

RESEARCH SERIES

We are passionate about performance and obsessed with the potential of organizations, groups and teams. While our work is primarily with senior leaders in blue chip organizations, we have made a commitment to make our applied research widely accessible to all. To this end we have published our frameworks and tools in a series of 6 books available to all who share our passion for unlocking the complexity of performance.

GROWTH PITSTOP™

The Growth Pitstop™ presents 4 Speed Tests from the racetrack to powerfully communicate the latest research into the requirements of accelerating business growth. It highlights growing evidence that sustained and profitable growth depends on cross-functional collaboration, or the ability of senior leaders to work like an effective pit team.

Format:	Paperback	ISBN:	978-1-907725-04-3
Pages:	609	Date:	June 2016

'An actionable agenda that managers can use for accelerating growth.'
Prof. Frank Cespedes, Harvard

PITSTOP TO PERFORM TOOL KITS™

There is a toolkit to help you
unlock performance gains for
each aspect of design and
dynamics in the Pitstop Meta-
model™.

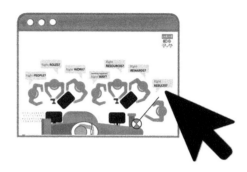

Available online these
incorporate the latest insights
from social psychology, behavioural economics, organizational
design and business leadership. Find out more at:

www.GrowthPitstop.com/shop

TEAMS DON'T WORK™

A wake-up call for teams, this book catalogues the
extent of team underperformance.   Building on
'Pitstop to Perform' it calls for a new language of
teams and presents a comprehensive model of
team performance which integrates the latest
research, as well as benchmarking data from 900 teams.

Format:	Paperback	ISBN:	978-1-907725-07-4
Pages:	220	Date:	Jan. 2018 (pre-release)

THE REVENUE TRACK™

'The Revenue Track™' links strategy (the stuff of The Growth Pitstop™) with implementation to tackle the execution challenge. Continuing the racing theme, it takes your growth machine onto the track (or into the marketplace) to execute its  strategy for growth. It explores the cross-functional; capabilities, processes and systems to acquire and retain customers.

Format:	Hardback (color)	ISBN:	978-1-907725-03-6
Pages:	500	Date:	May 2016

THE B2B SALES REVOLUTION™

'The B2B Sales Revolution' reveals the full complexity of corporate buying and presents a compendium of best practice buyer-friendly tools to be at each stage of the Revenue Track™.

Format:	Hardback	ISBN:	978-1-907725-00-5
Pages:	347	Date:	2010

Other titles by Ray Collis and John O Gorman include;

- 'B2B 'QuickWin B2B Sales' (ISBN: 978-1904887485)
- 'Selling in the Clouds' (ISBN: 9781907725012).

REFERENCES & BIBLIOGRAPHY

1 Michael Schumacher interviewed by Jonathan Noble in 2002 related in Daly, D. 'Race to Win: How to Become a Complete Champion Driver,' Motorbooks, 2008.

2 Jean Alesi, French racing driver, quoted on BrainyQuote. Link: http://www.brainyquote.com/quotes/quotes/j/jeanalesi331976.html

3 The Net Promoter Score is a management tool that can be used to gauge the loyalty of a firm's customer relationships. It is (according to Wikipedia) a registered trademark of Fred Reichheld, Bain & Company, and Satmetrix.

4 Taken from another book in this series called 'Growth Pitstop', by Ray Collis and John O Gorman, ASG Group Press 2016.

5 Indeed, the big question goes to the core of some of the hottest topics in psychology at this time: (i) Growth Mindset, (ii) Grit, (iii) Psychological safety and (iv) Psychological well-being. References: (i) Carol Dweck, 'Growth Mindset: The New Psychology of Success', Ballantine Books, 2007. (ii) Angela Duckworth, 'Grit: The Power of Passion and Perseverance', Vermillion, 2017. (iii) Amy C. Edmondson, 'Teaming: How Organizations Learn, Innovate, and Compete in the Knowledge Economy', Jossey-Bass Pfeiffer, 2014. (iv) Explore the latest research on Psychological Well-being and why it matters in 'Teams Don't Work' by Ray Collis and John O Gorman, ASG Group Press.

6 Based on pitstop research program data from 900 teams (see Appendix).

7 This is in line with the long-established portfolio approach to planning and strategy. As pointed out in another book in this series, called 'Growth Pitstop', 'Strategists have long viewed the performance of an organization as resting on how it manages its portfolio of business units, right down to the level of its different products aimed at different markets or segments. The view is that 'a one size fits all' approach does not work when it comes to planning or strategy.

8 See for example Patrick Viguerie, Sven Smit & Mehrdad Baghai, 'The Granularity of Growth: How to Identify the Sources of Growth and Drive Enduring Company Performance', Marshall Cavendish, 2008.

9 'Corporate-level strategy is the vehicle for allocating resources among all of the business units...' according to Larry Bossidy, Ram Charan & Charles Burck, 'Execution: The Discipline of Getting Things Done (Updated)', Random House Business Books, 2011.

10 A business unit or team has to be important, for its performance to matter. So, on a scale of 1-10 (where 10 = essential to success and 1 = inconsequential) how important is the team you have chosen. If it does not rate 7 or higher, then the BIG question becomes less important. There is little point asking the BIG question whose performance matters little to the success of the leader or the organization.

11 In this respect the 100% (full potential) shown on the line below the BIG question is often not an idealized external standard, but rather a subjective internal standard.

12 Later in the book will explore a range of structural factors – labelled 'design' - that impact on performance.

13 This highlights the link between home and work, as well as between well-being and performance.

14 For example performance reviews and incentives are applied at the level of the individual, with little consideration given to collaborative performance or team-based incentives. As Franz puts it: 'Too many organizations organize teams and then rely on individual goals and reward systems'. See: Timothy M. Franz, 'Group Dynamics and Team Interventions: Understanding and Improving Team Performance', Wiley-Blackwell, 2012.

15 The performance of any individual cannot be seen in isolation of the cultural environment of their organization and any groups or teams to which they belong. The social dimension of performance is explored in another book in this series called 'Teams Don't Work' by Ray Collis and John O Gorman.

16 There is an innate tendency to overestimate the impact of the individual on performance and underestimate the impact of all other factors. This bias is called the Fundamental Misattribution Error. See for example Daniel Kahneman, 'Thinking, Fast and Slow', Penguin, 2011.

17 As Peter M. Senge puts it: 'When placed in the same system or structure, people, however different, tend to produce similar results.... The systems perspective tells us that we must look beyond individual mistakes or bad luck to understand important problems.' Source: Peter M. Senge, 'The Fifth Discipline: The Art and Practice of The Learning Organization,' Doubleday; Revised and Updated edition, 2007.

18 Systems thinking requires looking beyond the person or event to the underlying systematic factors that produce particular patterns of results.

19 Jim Collins, 'Good to Great: Why Some Companies Make the Leap...And Others Don't,' HarperBusiness, 2001. The quote continues: '...leaders [in the

most successful companies] look in the mirror to apportion responsibility, never blaming bad luck when things go poorly.'

20 Davidai, Shai & Gilovich, Thomas, 'The headwinds/tailwinds asymmetry: An availability bias in assessments of barriers and blessings', Journal of Personality and Social Psychology, Vol 111(6), Dec 2016, 835-851.

21 Bentley, R. 'Speed Secrets: Professional Race Driving Techniques,' Motorbooks, 1998.

22 Jenson Button,'Life to the Limit: My Autobiography', Blink Publishing (19 Oct. 2017)

23 Angela Duckworth, 'Grit: The Power of Passion and Perseverance', Vermillion, 2017.

24 Managers with Type A personalities tend to be more competitive, stressed and time scarce – behaviors that leave them prone to coronary problems. This Type A behavior (TAB) afflicts over three quarters of all urban American males. See Meyer Friedman, 'Type a Behavior: Its Diagnosis and Treatment, Springer Science & Business Media, 31 Oct 1996 - Medical.

25 Performance and well-being are 'two sides of the same coin' as pointed out in 'Teams Don't Work' by Ray Collis & John O Gorman, ASG Group Press 2018 (pre-release).

26 Ayrton Senna quoted on http://www.f1-grandprix.com/?page_id=28278

27 While the issue of performance often focuses on specific individuals who are either high performers and poor performers, we know today that individual performance cannot be separated from group performance. While adding a high performer to a team can cause everybody to 'raise their game', a poor performer can have the reverse effect.

28 Explore the latest research on Psychological Well-being and why it matters in 'Teams Don't Work' by Ray Collis and John O Gorman. There you will see that 'Psychological Well-being is often described by words such as 'thriving' or 'flourishing'. This embraces the notion of making progress, realizing potential, functioning effectively and of course positive emotions, or feeling good'.

29 According to research these factors (energy, engagement and exploration) may account for as much as 50% of organizational success. See: Alex "Sandy" Pentland, 'The New Science of Building Great Teams', HBR, Apr. 2012.

30 We use the term 'safety' here to describe the concept of 'psychological safety' where people can open-up, share their views and be themselves without fear of isolation or retribution. See Amy C. Edmondson, 'Teaming:

How Organizations Learn, Innovate, and Compete in the Knowledge Economy', Jossey-Bass Pfeiffer, 2014.

31 The effectiveness of the dialog is a talisman for the level of cohesiveness, trust and respect, or mutual accountability within a team. Indeed, it is a key indicator of whether a supposed team is really a team at all (as opposed to a mere group or a crowd).

32 The P2P Score is the ratio of performance to potential and is determined by answering to the BIG Question in Section 1. This score becomes a metric (the P2P Metric™) when it is calculated using data captured by the Pitstop Analytics Platform.

33 Based on pitstop research program data from 900 teams (see Appendix).

34 The average P2P Score of 61% is just 2% points outside the 'Danger Zone' (i.e. <55%) as examined in Section 1. It is just inside the 'Normal Zone' (i.e. 55-74%).

35 Well-being is a measure of the vitality of a team and the extent to which it's members are thriving (1) or flourishing (2) within their present environment and set-up. (1) Gretchen Spreitzer & Christine Porath, 'Creating Sustainable Performance', HBR, Jan-Feb. 2012. (2) Martin Seligman, 'Flourish: The Tanner Lectures on Human Values Delivered at The Tanner Lectures on Human Values Delivered at e University of Michigan October 7, 2010; 'Flourish: Positive Psychology and Positive Interventions.'

36 'There has to be an economic justification for well-being. It is not corporate altruism – well-being is linked to business profitability and performance in a multiplicity of ways. These include increased engagement, reduced absenteeism and lower rates of staff turnover.' Source: Ray Collis & John O Gorman, ASG Group Press 2018 (pre-release).

37 Remember you set a goal for the % of your team's full potential exploited at the close of Section 1. So, take this opportunity to refer back to what you wrote there

38 The challenges associated with traditional performance management are explored in another book in the pitstop series called 'Growth Pitstop', Ray Collis and John O Gorman, ASG Group Press 2016.

39 Who is responsible for exploiting the potential of an organization or team? For example, is it the role of the CEO, the senior leadership team, Human Resources or Learning & Development? Does the responsibility for bringing performance and potential into equilibrium reside in one function, or is it a distributed responsibility - a part of every manager's and indeed everybody's job?

40 Much of the potential within an organization or team is hidden. It is not listed on the balance sheet, detailed in shareholder reports, or spelt out in employee records. Moreover, it can be difficult to measure - take for example the culture of the corporation or the dynamics of a team. Yet it is an organisation greatest resource - more valuable than additional production capacity, buildings or plant.

41 We have long held the view that there is no magic bullet or simple solution to the challenge of unlocking the potential of an organization or team. The answer is not to be found in traditional approaches to performance management, stand-alone HR initiatives, training programmes or team-building events. These may have a role to play, but there must be more. Performance is a complex jig-saw with many parts. No one discipline has all the answers. Creating the full picture requires looking beyond the idealized strategy and latest organizational design fad and recognizing that the workplace as a complex adaptive social system. Hence the requirement of integrating the traditional disciplines of management, strategy and organizational design, with insights from the exciting new fields of social psychology and behavioral economics.

42 This is based on pitstop research which identifies 186 performance variables and parameters. For over a decade we have cataloged, studied, classified and measured the barriers to peak performance in all their real-world complexity.

43 Remember the 4 tests that accompanied the BIG question in Section 1. These included the ability to have an effective dialog about performance and the ability to take action and adjust as a result. Also included was a test of energy or engagement around the topic of performance and the ability to measure and track performance. Leaders and teams who struggled with these tests around the BIG question will certainly struggle to identify and tackle the barriers to performance.

44 The effectiveness of teams is often explored in terms of Inputs and Outputs, or to be more precise an Input Process Output (I-P-O) model. The process is how team members 'interact with each other to accomplish the work' - see: Marks MA, Mathieu JE, Zaccaro SJ. 2001, 'A temporally based framework and taxonomy of team processes', Academy of Management Review 2001, Vol. 26, No. 3, 356-376.

45 In a Deloitte survey more than half of executives said that their organization's approach to performance management neither drives employee engagement or high performance. Quoted in Martin Reeves, Knut Haanaes & Janmejaya Sinha, 'Your Strategy Needs a Strategy: How to Choose and Execute the Right Approach', Harvard Business Review Press, 2015.

46 According to Mercer's 2013 Global Performance Management Survey Report, managers struggle in particular to: have candid performance dialog (33%) and to link performance to development planning (48%), providing career development coaching and direction (59%) – figures shown indicate percentage rating skills as 'marginal' in each area.

47 Systems thinking requires looking beyond the person or event to the underlying systematic factors that produce particular patterns of results.

48 Behind the Pitstop Analytics™ platform is a complex algorithm that scientifically identifies, models, measures and predicts performance losses, gains and risks within organizations, business units and teams. See Appendix.

[49] Michael Schumacher in an interview with "F1™ Racing" magazine January 2000. Source: http://www.formula1-dictionary.net/set_up.html
50 Daniel Kahneman, 'Thinking, Fast and Slow', Penguin, 2011

51 Performance losses affect not just the task effectiveness of teams, but also their decision smarts, social health and development potential.

52 It impacts on all 4 dimensions of team performance: Task, Decision, Social and Development. This relates to the view of performance 'in the round' examined in the 'lollipop model' of team performance as part of the pitstop meta-model.

53 As examined at the bottom of the pitstop meta-model Social Health encompasses the relations, behaviors and interactions among the members of an organization/team. It can also be defined by the 'culture' of an organization and is tied to 8 critical behaviors in the model.

54 How the task performance and social health are intertwined is examined in the sections exploring the bottom of the pitstop meta-model.

55 Heidi Grant Halvorson Ph.D. & E. Tory Higgins Ph.D., 'Focus: Use Different Ways of Seeing the World for Success and Influence', Hudson Street Press, 2013.

56 Of course, there are certain to be other losses deriving from the underperformance of any team including the impact on key projects, strategies and priorities. However, the calculation of the running cost of a team provides one of the least contentious means of calculating performance losses.

57 The importance of team potency is widely accepted, see for example; BRADLEY L. KIRKMAN, BENSON ROSEN, PAUL E. TESLUK & CRISTINA B. GIBSON, 'THE IMPACT OF TEAM EMPOWERMENT ON VIRTUAL TEAM

PERFORMANCE: THE MODERATING ROLE OF FACE-TO-FACE INTERACTION', Academy of Management Journal 2004, Vol. 47, No. 2, 175–192.

58 See for example, Barry J Moltz, 'Bounce!: Failure, Resiliency, and Confidence to Achieve Your Next Great Success', John Wiley & Sons, 2008.

59 'Jump the curve' is a reference to Charles Handy's idea that success follow an S curve (the sigmoid curve), those organizations that sustain success maintain a continuous upward progress by jump from one curve to the next. See: Charles Handy,'The Empty Raincoat: Making Sense of the Future, Random House Business', 1995.

60 'A Tale of Two Cities' was first published by Charles Dickens in 1859.

61 As Sam Michael, Sporting Director, McLaren Mercedes puts it All of F1™ is about teamwork is not about an individual sport anymore. Sam Michael interviewed on 'The science behind F1 pit stops with McLaren and GSK'. Link: https://www.youtube.com/watch?v=Qh3DOGVrgBE

62 Michael Schumacher – a Formula One™ legend and winner of 7 Championships – source 'Quotes from Formula 1' Link: http://f1quotes.tumblr.com/post/34167189201

63 McKinsey argues that managers spend most of their time focused on strategies, systems and structures (that is the 'hard stuff') within their organizations.   However, this accounts for just 47% of success. The rest (called 'soft' or 'organizational health' accounts for 53%63. Source: Scott Keller & Colin Price, 'Beyond Performance: How Great Organizations Build Ultimate Competitive Advantage', Wiley 2011.

64 Harvard research suggests that patterns of communication among teams (in particular levels of energy, exploration and engagement) account for as much as 50% of the performance gap between the worst and the best. Alex "Sandy" Pentland, 'The New Science of Building Great Teams', HBR, Apr. 2012.

65 The development of the model, including the concepts of mental modelling and cognitive re-framing are examined in Growth Pitstop™ by Ray Collis and John O Gorman, ASG Press, 2016.

66 Find out about the history of the model and the secrets of its design in the Growth Pitstop™ book. Ray Collis & John O Gorman, Growth Pitstop, ASG Group Press, 2016.

67 Chris Ertel & Lisa Kay Solomon, 'Moments of Impact: How to Design Strategic Conversations That Accelerate Change,' 2014.

68 For more on how F1™ has shaped the ordinary motor car see:
- 'Top 10 Everyday Car Technologies That Came From Racing', BY JAMIE PAGE DEATON on How Stuff Works.com, link:
http://auto.howstuffworks.com/under-the-hood/trends-innovations/top-10-car-tech-from-racing.htm

- 'F1 tech still shaping tomorrow's transport' By Russell Hotten and Matthew Wall, BBC Business News, 9 March 2015. Link:
http://www.bbc.com/news/business-31096844

69 Sam Michael, Sporting Director, McLaren Mercedes, interviewed on 'The science behind F1 pit stops with McLaren and GSK'. Link:
https://www.youtube.com/watch?v=Qh3DOGVrgBE

70 Gallagher, M., 'The Business of Winning: Strategic Success from the Formula One™ Track to the Boardroom,' Kogan Page, 2014.

71 Keith Collantine, 'A brief history of pit stops in F1' on F1fanatic.com 29th August 2008, Link: http://www.f1fanatic.co.uk/2008/08/29/a-brief-history-of-pit-stops-in-f1-video/

72 Frederick Taylor is the father of Scientific Management who with a clipboard and stopwatch introduced the concept of efficient production processes. Henry Ford is the father of the production line and efficient mass production. Edward Deming developed the principles of Ford and Taylor to set the principles that underpinned world class manufacturing and the emergence of global Japanese brands such as Toyota and Sony.

73 Gordon Murray is the father of the modern day pitstop. In this quote he recalls the process of re-engineering the pitstop as in this extract 'Motor Sport Greats...in conversation' by Simon Taylor, Haynes Publishing, 2013.

74 Richard Hackman defines a 'real team' in line with the following criteria; it is doing a job for a team, there is real interdependence between team members, as well as a level of autonomy/accountability. The team is bounded in terms of membership and has some element of stability. See: Richard Hackman, 'Groups That Work (and Those That Don't): Creating Conditions for Effective Teamwork', Jossey-Bass, 2007.

75 Sam Michael, Sporting Director, McLaren Mercedes, interviewed on 'The science behind F1 pit stops with McLaren and GSK'. Link:
https://www.youtube.com/watch?v=Qh3DOGVrgBE

76 Keith Collantine, 'A brief history of pit stops in F1' on F1fanatic.com 29th August 2008, Link: http://www.f1fanatic.co.uk/2008/08/29/a-brief-history-of-pit-stops-in-f1-video/

77 Derek Daly is a retired F1™ Racer who competed in 64 Grand Prix races. Here is author of 'Race to Win' & 'How to Become a Complete Champion Driver'.

78 'Co-acting groups are barely groups at all' according to J. Richard Hackman, where 'members usually work in proximity to one another and have the same supervisor. But each member has an individual job to do, and that job's completion does not depend on what the others do'. See

J. Richard Hackman, 'Groups That Work (and Those That Don't): Creating Conditions for Effective Teamwork', Jossey-Bass, 2007.

79 Morten Hansen, 'Collaboration: How Leaders Avoid the Traps, Build Common Ground, and Reap Big Results', Harvard Business Review Press, 2009.

80 Douglas Smith & Jon Katzenbach, 'The Wisdom of Teams: Creating the High-Performance Organization', Harvard Business Review Press, 2015.

81 In the world of business, the word team is overused and even abused. In everyday conversation 'team' is a catch all term used to describe any collaborative effort, regardless of whether it is a committee, a working group, or anything else. Moreover, the term 'teamwork' is used to describe a cultural aspiration - you might for example hear managers say; 'in this organization we are all one big team'. In addressing the issue of team performance getting more precise with language is an important first step. Most teams within organizations are teams in name only. They are groups of individuals – just like at the bottom of the meta model - where the whole often falls considerably short of the sum of its parts. Those managers who are 'in the know' reserve the words 'team' or 'real team' for a particular form of collaborative endeavor - one that promises more in terms of performance (as at the top of the model), but also demands more in terms of structure, leadership, resources and support. They don't expect groups or committees to perform to the same level as teams, moreover they don't expect to have to invest so heavily in their development either.

82 Gordon Curphy & Robert Hogan, 'The Rocket Model: Practical Advice for Building High Performing Teams,' Hogan Press, 2012.

83 Ruth Wageman, Debra A. Nunes, James A. Burruss, J. Richard Hackman, 'Senior Leadership Teams: What It Takes to Make Them Great (Leadership for the Common Good)', Harvard Business Review Press, 2008.

84 John Carrey, Lotus Race Team Pit Crew, interviewed for 'Lotus F1 Pitstop Practice - One Second in F1™' by CNBC International. Link: https://www.youtube.com/watch?v=iuqRVjPPEC0

85 J. Richard Hackman, 'Groups That Work (and Those That Don't): Creating Conditions for Effective Teamwork', Jossey-Bass, 2007.

86 Ruth Wageman, Debra A. Nunes, James A. Burruss, J. Richard Hackman, 'Senior Leadership Teams: What It Takes to Make Them Great (Leadership for the Common Good)', Harvard Business Review Press, 2008.

87 Ruth Wageman, Debra A. Nunes, James A. Burruss, J. Richard Hackman, 'Senior Leadership Teams: What It Takes to Make Them Great (Leadership for the Common Good)', Harvard Business Review Press, 2008.

88 Rich Karlgaard & Michael S. Malone, 'Team Genius: The New Science of High-Performing Organizations', HarperBusiness, 2015.

89 We use the broad classification 'design school' to refer to the work of authors such as Richard Hackman, Ruth Wageman, Michael A. West, Douglas Smith & John Katzenbach, whose primary (but not exclusive) focus was on team set-up and design. That can be contrasted with those authors primarily concerned with the ability to collaborate effectively / behaviors of effective teamwork, including Patrick Leinconi, Peter Senge, Amy Edmondson and Margaret Heffernan. For convenience we classify the latter as the 'dynamics school'. The Pitstop Metamodel™ places equal emphasis on both perspectives of organizational/team performance.

90 The commissioning process is identified by Peter Hawkins as one of the 5 dimensions of high performing teams. See for example: Peter Hawkins, 'Leadership Team Coaching: Developing Collective Transformational Leadership', Kogan Page, 2014

91 Khoi Tu, 'Superteams: The Secrets of Stellar Performance from Seven Legendary Teams', Portfolio Penguin, 2012.

92 'Begin with the End in Mind' is one of Stephen Covey's 7 Habits of Highly Effective Managers it means 'to begin each day, task, or project with a clear vision of your desired direction and destination'. Source: Stephen R. Covey, 'The 7 Habits of Highly Effective People', Free Press, 1990.

93 As Daniel Kahneman put is: 'it is much easier, as well as far more enjoyable, to identify and label the mistakes of others than to recognize our own'. Source Daniel Kahneman, 'Thinking, Fast and Slow', Penguin, 2011.

94 Douglas Smith & Jon Katzenbach, 'The Wisdom of Teams: Creating the High-Performance Organization', Harvard Business Review Press, 2015.

95 'The Girl Power That Really Drives Formula One', Christian Sylt, Forbes, Aug. 1st 2016. Link: http://www.forbes.com/sites/csylt/2016/08/01/the-girl-power-that-really-drives-formula-one/#45418aed4f94

96 As Khoi Tu explains: 'The starting point of superteams is great individual talent. The only time brilliant, super-creative individuals will share the same room is when they have a common purpose.' See: Khoi Tu, 'Superteams: The Secrets of Stellar Performance from Seven Legendary Teams', Portfolio Penguin, 2012.

97 Pit Stop Feature by Williams F1 Team, https://www.youtube.com/watch?v=1CYsqHeylME

98 Michael A. West, 'Effective Teamwork: Practical Lessons from Organizational Research', Wiley-Blackwell, 2012.

99 Geoffrey M. Bellman and Kathleen D. Ryan in 'Extraordinary Groups: How Ordinary Teams Achieve Amazing Results', John Wiley & Sons, 2009.

100 J. Richard Hackman, 'Groups That Work (and Those That Don't): Creating Conditions for Effective Teamwork', Jossey-Bass, 2007.

101 Jay R. Galbraith, 'Designing Organizations: Strategy, Structure, and Process at the Business Unit and Enterprise Levels', Mar 2014

102 'Co-acting groups are barely groups at all' according to J. Richard Hackman, where 'members usually work in proximity to one another and have the same supervisor. But each member has an individual job to do, and that job's completion does not depend on what the others do'. See J. Richard Hackman, 'Groups That Work (and Those That Don't): Creating Conditions for Effective Teamwork', Jossey-Bass, 2007.

103 See Tom Peters, 'A Brief History of the 7-S ("McKinsey 7-S") Model'. Link: http://tompeters.com/docs/7SHistory.pdf. However, remember that as Peters says here "Hard is soft. Soft is hard." That is, it's the plans and the numbers that are often "soft". And the people and shared values and skills which are truly "hard"

104 Morten Hansen, 'Collaboration: How Leaders Avoid the Traps, Build Common Ground, and Reap Big Results', Harvard Business Review Press, 2009.

105 Patrick M. Lencioni is probably the number one exponent of Organizational health. See: Patrick M. Lencioni, 'The Advantage: Why Organizational Health Trumps Everything Else In Business,' Jossey-Bass, 2012.

106 Alex "Sandy" Pentland, 'The New Science of Building Great Teams', HBR, Apr. 2012.

107 Scott Keller & Colin Price, 'Beyond Performance: How Great Organizations Build Ultimate Competitive Advantage', Wiley 2011.

108 A Lencioni puts it: 'The single greatest advantage that any organization can achieve is organizational health. Yet it is ignored by most leaders even though it is simple, free and available to almost everybody who wants it'.

See: Patrick M. Lencioni, 'The Advantage: Why Organizational Health Trumps Everything Else In Business,' Jossey-Bass, 2012.

109 Patrick Lencioni, 'The Five Dysfunctions of a Team: A Leadership Fable', Jossey-Bass, 2002.

110 As Daniel Goleman puts it: 'Evolutionary theory holds that our ability to sense when we should be suspicious has been every bit as essential for human survival as our capacity for trust and cooperation'. See Daniel Goleman, 'Social Intelligence: The New Science of Human Relationships', Bantam, 2007.

111 Margaret Heffernan, 'Willful Blindness: Why We Ignore the Obvious', Simon & Schuster UK, 2012.

112 Amy C. Edmondson, 'Teaming: How Organizations Learn, Innovate, and Compete in the Knowledge Economy', Jossey-Bass Pfeiffer, 2014.

113 Amy C. Edmondson, 'Teaming: How Organizations Learn, Innovate, and Compete in the Knowledge Economy', Jossey-Bass Pfeiffer, 2014.

114 The use of the term dynamics links back to the concept of Group Dynamics as coined by Kurt Lewin in the middle of the last century. He defined groups as people connected to each other by social relationships and explored the social effects on behavior that resulted. See: Lewin, K. (1948). Resolving Social Conflicts: Selected Papers on Group Dynamics. New York: Harper and Row.

115 The use of the term dynamics is inspired by the application of systems thinking to social systems. To use Richmond's definition: 'Systems Thinking is the art and science of making reliable inferences about behavior by developing an increasingly deep understanding of underlying structure'. Source: Barry Richmond, 'System Dynamics/Systems Thinking: Let's Just Get On With It', paper delivered at the 1994 International Systems Dynamics Conference in Sterling, Scotland.

116 Manfred F. R. Kets de Vries, 'The Hedgehog Effect: The Secrets of Building High Performance Teams', Jossey-Bass, 2011.

117 Morten Hansen, 'Collaboration: How Leaders Avoid the Traps, Build Common Ground, and Reap Big Results', Harvard Business Review Press, 2009.

118 Interview with the late Prof. Richard Hackman by Diane Coutu, 'Why Teams Don't Work', HBR, May 2009. Link: https://hbr.org/2009/05/why-teams-dont-work

119 According to research by Strategy& (formerly Booz & Company) and The Katzenbach Centre, 84% of manages believe that culture is critical to business success, with 60% believing that it is more important than strategy or operating model. See: 'Culture & Change, Why Culture Matters and How it Makes Change Stick', Culture & Change Management Survey by Strategy& (formerly Booz & Company) and The Katzenbach Centre, 2013.

120 'Culture eats strategy for breakfast' is the often quoted saying, attributed to Peter Drucker, that is used to emphasize the power of culture and in particular its ability to block change.

121 Ken Favaro, 'Strategy or Culture: Which Is More Important?', Strategy + Business, S+B BLOGS Published: May 22, 2014. Link: http://www.strategy-business.com/blog/Strategy-or-Culture-Which-Is-More-Important?

122 According to the same research by Strategy& (formerly Booz & Company) and The Katzenbach Centre, 51% of managers think a major overhaul is needed in their culture while only one in three think that their company's culture is being managed effectively. See: 'Culture & Change, Why Culture Matters and How it Makes Change Stick', Culture & Change Management Survey by Strategy& (formerly Booz & Company) and The Katzenbach Centre, 2013.

123 As Katzenbach, Oelschlegel & Thomas put it: 'Made of instinctive, repetitive habits and emotional responses, culture can't be copied or easily pinned down'. Jon Katzenbach, Carolin Oelschlegel & James Thomas, '10 Principles of Organizational Culture', Strategy+Business, Feb. 2016, Link: http://www.strategy-business.com/article/10-Principles-of-Organizational-Culture

124 Michael D. Watkins, 'What Is Organizational Culture? And Why Should We Care?', HBR, MAY 15, 2013, Link: https://hbr.org/2013/05/what-is-organizational-culture

125 Jon Katzenbach, Laird Post, Aurelie Viriot, & Jonathan Gruber, 'Motivating behavior change: Boosting performance by mobilizing pride builders', Booz & Company: April 21, 2011.

126 Jon Katzenbach, Laird Post, Aurelie Viriot, & Jonathan Gruber, 'Motivating behavior change: Boosting performance by mobilizing pride builders', Booz & Company: April 21, 2011.

127 As Mankins & Garton put it: 'Successful individuals in a company exhibit a distinct behavioral signature, a common way of working that enables them to deliver high performance where others turn in mediocre results'. See: Michael C. Mankins & Eric Garton, 'Time, Talent, Energy: Overcome Organizational Drag and Unleash Your Teams Productive Power', Harvard Business Review Press, 2017.

128 Moreover, they are 'complex adaptive systems' according to Amy C. Edmondson, 'Teaming: How Organizations Learn, Innovate, and Compete in the Knowledge Economy', Jossey-Bass Pfeiffer, 2014.

129 Kets de Vries talks about 'the relational soup'; 'And while we are swimming in this soup, we tend to overlook the fact that team or group dynamics, when properly facilitated, can fuel efficient and effective individual and group actions and behavioral change'. Source: Manfred F. R. Kets de Vries, 'The Hedgehog Effect: The Secrets of Building High Performance Teams', Jossey-Bass, 2011.

130 Daniel Goleman uses the term 'emotional stew'; Everyone in a given workplace contributes to the emotional stew, the sum total of the moods that emerge as they interact through the workday. ...how we do our work, interact, and make each other feel adds to the overall emotional tone. Source: Daniel Goleman, 'Social Intelligence: The New Science of Human Relationships', Bantam, 2006.

131 The 'Lollipop Model' is a view of performance in the round, including Task, Social, Decision and Developmental aspects of a team. You will see the model in the Toolkit section of this book. The model is examined in more detail under Right Results in 'Pitstop for Performance' and is the subject of our other book 'Teams Don't Work' (see appendix).

132 Ken Favaro, 'Strategy or Culture: Which Is More Important?', Strategy + Business, S+B BLOGS Published: May 22, 2014. Link: http://www.strategy-business.com/blog/Strategy-or-Culture-Which-Is-More-Important?

133 As Katzenbach et al. put it: 'It's one thing to determine the critical few behaviors, but quite another to get your employees to adopt them. In most cases this cannot be done by decree, however desirable that might be'. See:

Jon Katzenbach, Laird Post, Aurelie Viriot, & Jonathan Gruber, 'Motivating behavior change: Boosting performance by mobilizing pride builders', Booz & Company: April 21, 2011.

134 Jon Katzenbach, Laird Post, Aurelie Viriot & Jonathan Gruber, 'Motivating behavior change: Boosting performance by mobilizing pride builders', Booz & Company: April 21, 2011.

135 Managers with Type A personalities tend to be more competitive, stressed and time scarce – behaviors that leave them prone to coronary problems. This Type A behavior (TAB) afflicts over three quarters of all urban American males. See Meyer Friedman, 'Type a Behavior: Its Diagnosis and Treatment, Springer Science & Business Media, 31 Oct 1996 - Medical.

136 J. P. Kotter, 'A Sense of Urgency,' Harvard Business Press, 2008.

137 Michael C. Mankins & Eric Garton, 'Time, Talent, Energy: Overcome Organizational Drag and Unleash Your Teams Productive Power', Harvard Business Review Press, 2017.

138 Morten Hansen, 'Collaboration: How Leaders Avoid the Traps, Build Common Ground, and Reap Big Results', Harvard Business Review Press, 2009.

139 Alex "Sandy" Pentland, 'The New Science of Building Great Teams', HBR, Apr. 2012. Link: https://hbr.org/2012/04/the-new-science-of-building-great-teams/ar/1

140 Gallagher, M., 'The Business of Winning: Strategic Success from the Formula One™ Track to the Boardroom,' Kogan Page, 2014.

141 Amy C. Edmondson, 'Teaming: How Organizations Learn, Innovate, and Compete in the Knowledge Economy', Jossey-Bass Pfeiffer, 2014.

142 James Kerr, 'Legacy – What the All Blacks Can Teach Us About The Business of Life', Constable, 2013.

143 Robert Kegan & Lisa Laskow Lahey, 'An Everyone Culture: Becoming a Deliberately Developmental Organization', Harvard Business Review Press, 2016.

144 Howard M. Guttman, 'Great Business Teams: Cracking the Code for Standout Performance', Wiley, 2008.

145 Howard M. Guttman, 'Great Business Teams: Cracking the Code for Standout Performance', Wiley, 2008.

146 Sebastian Vettel Quotes on AZ Quotes. Link: http://www.azquotes.com/author/15073-Sebastian_Vettel

147 Monte Carlo, Monaco circuit information from F1Fanatic. Link: http://www.f1fanatic.co.uk/f1-information/going-to-a-race/monte-carlo-circuit-information/

148 Lewis Hamilton quoted in The Daily Mail as referenced on Planet F1. Link: http://www.planetf1.com/driver/3213/9363275/Hamilton-Only-the-first-matters

149 Ian Blakey & John Day, 'Challenging Coaching: Going beyond traditional coaching to face the FACTS', Nicholas Brealey Publishing, 2012.

150 A.G. Lafley & Roger L. Martin, 'Playing to Win: How Strategy Really Works,' HBR Press, 2013.

151 For example as Brian Tracey says: 'The only real limitation on your abilities is the level of your desires. If you want it badly enough, there are no limits on what you can achieve'. Source: Brian Tracy, 'Maximum Achievement,' Simon & Schuster, 1993

152 Richard P. Rumelt, 'Good/Bad Strategy,' Profile Books, 2012.

153 J. P. Kotter, 'A Sense of Urgency,' Harvard Business Press, 2008.

154 You will see the 'Lollipop Model' in the Toolkit section of this book. The model is examined in more detail under Right Results in 'Pitstop for Performance' and is the subject of our other book 'Teams Don't Work' (see appendix).

155 Neel Doshi & Lindsay McGrego, 'Primed to Perform - The Science of High-Performing Cultures Demystified', HarperBusiness, 2015.

156 Mehrdad Baghai, Stephen Coley, and David White, 'The Alchemy of Growth,' New York: Perseus Publishing, 1999.

157 Hayagreeva Rao & Robert I. Sutton, 'Scaling up Excellence', Random House, 2014

158 Sydney Finkelstein, 'Superbosses: How Exceptional Leaders Master the Flow of Talent', Portfolio, 2016.

159 Cynthia Montgomery, 'The Strategist: Be the Leader Your Business Needs,' HarperBusiness, 2012.

160 Heidi Grant Halvorson Ph.D. & E. Tory Higgins Ph.D., 'Focus: Use Different Ways of Seeing the World for Success and Influence', Hudson Street Press, 2013.

161 Peter M. Senge, 'The Fifth Discipline: The Art and Practice of The Learning Organization,' Doubleday; Revised and Updated edition, 2006.

162 Quotes from Juan Manuel Fangio on Brainy Quote. Link: http://www.brainyquote.com/quotes/authors/j/juan_manuel_fangio.html

163 Cynthia Montgomery, 'The Strategist: Be the Leader Your Business Needs,' HarperBusiness, 2012.

164 The Kaplan and Norton Balanced Scorecard typically compliments financial measures with operational indicators relating to customer

satisfaction, internal processes, and learning/improvement. See: Robert S. Kaplan & David P. Norton, 'The Balanced Scorecard: Measures That Drive Performance', HBR Jul-Aug. 2005.

165 This view of team performance in the round (Task, Social, Decision and Development) is examined in the book 'Teams Don't Work' by Ray Collis and John O Gorman, ISBN: 978-1-907725-07-4.

166 Quotes from Michael Schumacher on Brainy Quote. Link: ttp://www.brainyquote.com/quotes/authors/m/michael_schumacher.html

167 Aryton Senna Society on Facebook. Link: https://www.facebook.com/ayrtonsennasociety/

168 Reid Hoffman and Ben Casnocha, 'The Alliance: Managing Talent in the Networked Age', HBR Press, 2014.

169 Maslow, A.H. (1943). "Pyschological Review 50 (4) 370–96 - A theory of human motivation"

170 'Motivating Salespeople – How managers Can Get it Wrong', by Ray Collis, July 31 2014. Link: http://salesstrategypitstop.theasggroup.com/2014/07/31/motivating-salespeople-how-managers-get-it-wrong/

171 Garry Hammel, 'What Matters Now: How to win in a world of relentless change...'Jossey-Boss, 2012.

172 Reid Hoffman and Ben Casnocha, The Alliance: Managing Talent in the Networked Age, Harvard Business Review Press, 2014.

173 Sebastian Vettel Quotes on AZ Quotes. Link: http://www.azquotes.com/author/15073-Sebastian_Vettel

174 Geoffrey M. Bellman and Kathleen D. Ryan, 'Extraordinary Groups: How Ordinary Teams Achieve Amazing Results', John Wiley & Sons, 2009.

175 Amy Wilkinson, 'The Creator's Code: The Six Essential Skills of Extraordinary Entrepreneurs', Simon & Schuster, 2015.

176 Margaret J. Wheatley, 'Turning to One Another: Simple Conversations to Restore Hope to the Future', Berrett-Koehler Publishers, 2009.

177 Colm Chapman, quoted in Karl Ludvigsen's book 'Colin Chapman: Inside the Innovator.' Referenced online at: http://jalopnik.com/5840611/colin-chapmans-simple-and-chilling-definition-of-a-formula-one-race-car

178 References in respect of: (i) Growth Mindset and (ii) Psychological safety. See: (i) Carol Dweck, 'Growth Mindset: The New Psychology of

Success', Ballantine Books, 2007 (ii) Amy C. Edmondson, 'Teaming: How Organizations Learn, Innovate, and Compete in the Knowledge Economy', Jossey-Bass Pfeiffer, 2014.

Lightning Source UK Ltd.
Milton Keynes UK
UKHW05f1557020218

317274UK00002B/7/P